55

ANATOMY OF A FRAUD INVESTIGATION

ANATOMY OF A FRAUD INVESTIGATION

FROM DETECTION TO PROSECUTION

Stephen Pedneault

WILEY

John Wiley & Sons, Inc.

Library of Congress Cataloging-in-Publication Data:

Pedneault, Stephen, 1966-
  Anatomy of a fraud investigation : from detection to prosecution/Stephen Pedneault.
    p. cm.
  Includes bibliographical references and index.
  ISBN 978-0-470-56047-1 (cloth)
  1. Fraud. 2. Fraud investigation. I. Title.
  HV6691.P43 2010
  363.25'963—dc22

                                                                2009035916

Printed in the United States of America.

10 9 8 7 6 5 4 3 2 1

With deep appreciation and love, for my parents, Gerry and Dot. Your personal sacrifices gave me so many opportunities growing up. Your strong work ethic, sense of values, and ideals created the foundation for the man I strive to be today.

Thank you,
—Steve

CONTENTS

ACKNOWLEDGMENTS

To my family, who allow me the time I need to accomplish so much in so little time, who may not know how much I value the time we spend together (away from my work), and who provide me with the spirit and energy needed during my often long hours of work.

To my friends and trusted advisors, who at times think I am crazy with the number of projects and endeavors I undertake simultaneously, yet continue to support me and my decisions anyway.

To Helen Koven, my friend and publicist, whose vision and drive is nothing less than that of Walt Disney himself, the brains behind the curtain just beyond the spotlight, continually demonstrating her experience and expertise in marketing and promotion.

To Timothy Burgard, Stacey Rivera, Lisa Vuoncino, and all the folks at Wiley who have been a delight to work with in publishing my first book, *Fraud 101*, and who have extended themselves once again by creating a second opportunity for my writing.

To Lt. Albert J. Kerling, East Hartford Police Department (retired), who gave so much of his time and energy to the police explorer program, which provided me with much of my criminal justice knowledge and experience, and created the backdrop for my career decisions.

And to the Association of Certified Fraud Examiners, the premier international organization that provides superior educational opportunities directed to prevent fraud as well as investigate fraud, leading the world on their crusade to bring fraudulent activity back to a controlled level.

INTRODUCTION

When the case became available to the public, journalists flocked to the station to read the blotter details regarding the arrest. A well-known executive with strong community ties was charged with a financial crime involving a very reputable non-profit organization. As the story broke that day to the public, it appeared in a local newspaper and on a local television station. A camera crew went to the suspect's house to capture a distant glimpse of someone looking out an upstairs window for the six o'clock news. Reporters fanned out to talk with neighbors about how great the suspect was, and how surprised they were to hear the news. Nothing sells better than unplanned reactions to "shock-and-awe" reporting.

When the printed story came out later that day, it was consistent with so many others similarly reported, and read as follows:

Controller Charged With Embezzling from Non-Profit Agency

James Smith, 43, was arrested yesterday on charges that he pilfered hundreds of thousands of dollars from his employer over the course of several years. Smith turned himself in to local authorities accompanied by his attorney after learning that police had secured a warrant for his arrest.

Smith started at Crestview as an accounting manager and rose through the ranks to become their controller. A surprise audit revealed Smith used the organization's credit cards for personal expenses in support of his lavish lifestyle, including trips he took throughout the world. Funds intended for Crestview were diverted into a bank account opened by Smith that he allegedly used to pay the credit card activity each month.

Shortly after the discovery, Smith was placed on administrative leave. As part of the negotiations for a potential plea deal, Smith purportedly agreed to initially return $78,000 and make restitution to Crestview for the full amount of their loss.

(Continued)

(*Continued*)

    Smith was released on a $100,000 bond and is scheduled to appear in court next month on March 29th. No one answered the phone at Smith's residence, and messages left for his attorney went unreturned.

The story appeared that day, and nothing further was ever heard again on the matter until the day of Mr. Smith's sentencing. Even then the media's attention was limited to a very small follow-up article revealing no new or additional details about the case. No television crews were at the courthouse, and no reporters went to Mr. Smith's neighbors for comment and reaction to the sentence handed down. There was nothing reported from the media because it had become old news and there were other things happening in the world worthy of attention.

There was nothing unique about this story. In fact, the only thing that was even remotely unique was that it initially appeared in earlier stories at all. Most fraud cases, especially thefts and embezzlements, never even make it to the public's eye for many reasons. Statistically, one in nine matters ever appear in the media, and I know from my own personal experience that one is nine is pretty accurate.

Cases are often resolved quietly under confidential circumstances, and when they are reported for public access, they appear in abbreviated fashion. The lack of stories and details give readers little or no means of learning how these types of cases occur or are discovered, investigated, and ultimately resolved. For experienced and inexperienced fraud professionals alike, there is little available to initially learn or keep abreast of the latest fraud tactics. Readers want details. I want details. The problem is I never find them.

The stories and cases that actually do grab the media's attention merely report the end result of weeks, months, and even years of investigative procedures. Due to space, time, and cost limitations, only select highlights or points are typically included to tell the story. Along the lines of Sergeant Joe Friday's approach from the television series *Dragnet*, the story omits all the rich details in exchange for the ''Just the facts, Ma'am'' writing style.

What about how the case came to light in the first place? How about the stakeout and raid used to secure much of the evidence that was instrumental in leading to the arrest? Who were the individuals behind the scene putting the case together, sifting through ledgers, canceled checks, and other records that comprised a mountain of evidence? Who handled all that information, and where does one store that kind of evidence? What else was found during the investigation, and where did it lead in the case? Who were the witnesses, and did the suspect act alone or with the assistance of an accomplice? Were computer forensics involved, and what was discovered on their computers? We want the juicy details that are next to never reported.

The rich details are rarely found in the news stories, and are lacking in most books published on fraud and fraud investigations, yet the *who, what, where, when, how,* and *why* are the very details sought by readers of all levels, within and beyond the fraud profession. There is such a need to tell the full tales of the unsung heroes (if you will) who bring their expertise and experience into an investigation to help solve a particular matter or crime. I know from my own experience that getting paid for the work is a motivator for many, but many fraud investigators like myself simply enjoy the challenge of piecing together a fraud investigation. Persisting on a minor detail that leads to the discovery of major information, or listening to a witness's or suspect's story or explanation, only to systematically lead them through an unraveling at their own hands, is what drives me.

These are the details that make fraud investigative work interesting and challenging—articulating the thought process from beginning to end. What led to the need to raid the location? What was it like showing up unexpectedly and taking over? How did the employees react? How did you deal with all that information, including that of the employees' computers? And why did the media never learn about the whole thing going on right under their noses?

This book is intended to fill the void created by omitting the rich details, and provide in as much detail as possible the steps and measures used in an actual fraud investigation, starting from the time the initial allegation was received right through to the final resolution of the matter.

While the facts specific to the case have been changed to protect the identities of all parties involved, the basis of this book is an actual fraud investigation based on firsthand knowledge of all the details. This is particularly applicable when the nature and amount of the theft is first identified. While the fraud scheme may seem unusual for the organization depicted in the story, the number of transactions, dollar amounts, fraud methodology, and other details are factual, based on the actual victim organization.

In order to provide more to the reader beyond simply sharing an interesting story, fraud facts, learning points, and key considerations have been added throughout the book relevant to the sections of the investigation, enabling the reader not only to learn critical fraud-related issues at each stage of an investigation, but also to relate the materials to the actual case discussed throughout the book.

I hope you enjoy the case involving Mr. Smith and Crestview.

CHAPTER 1

FIRST INDICATIONS
(THEY'RE DOING WHAT?)

It was a bit after 5:00 P.M. on a Friday afternoon. The sun was out and still strong, and I was looking forward to ending my busy week by relaxing outside in my reclining lawn chair, soaking up the warm evening air. I had just pulled into my driveway and started to unload my client files and briefcase from the trunk of my car when I heard my cell phone ringing. As it rang, I fumbled through my pockets trying to find it, only to realize I had left it on the front seat of the car. Of course, by then the fourth ring had finished, and the caller went into my voicemail. I carried the files into the house and returned back out to retrieve my phone and see if the caller left a message. Although the missed call number looked familiar, I couldn't place it.

I retrieved the message and recognized the voice immediately. It was the chief financial officer of a well-known non-profit organization called Crestview that I had done work for in the past. I knew right then before I concentrated on his message that if he was calling me on a Friday night after 5:00, something big was happening or about to happen. His message went like this:

"Steve, Tim Hill. How are you? Sorry to bother you on a weekend, but I need to talk with you, the sooner the better. Any chance you can call me back tonight when you receive this message, I would appreciate it. I will be here late tonight, and you can reach me anytime on my cell phone. My number is 806-510-1234. I would really like to talk with you as soon as possible."

I took out a pen and pad from my car and listened to his message a second time, this time writing down his cell number. I

1

walked into the house, checked in with my wife and kids, and let them know I needed to return a very important call to a client that I just received. Then I walked back outside, straight over to my front steps, and sat down, knowing the call might take a while and that the sun lasted the longest in that area of my yard. I knew once I returned Tim's call that my plans for a restful night and weekend were going to change.

• • •

I dialed his number and he answered immediately. After asking each other what was new and how things were going, I asked Tim how I could help. He asked me if I had a few minutes, or did I want to call him back later in the evening when he could spend a few minutes with me on the phone. I told him now would be fine. Tim provided me with the following details:

"I received information this week that a controller in one of our divisions could be stealing money from the organization. While the person who provided me with this information wished to remain anonymous and provided little to no details, I told them there was little I could do unless they provided me with more details and possibly examples of how the controller was stealing the funds. Reluctantly, they managed to get a copy of a credit card statement used by the controller that is paid through their division's checking account. Once I saw the statement, I realized I had a big problem due to the high volume of personal charges made on the card in the one month alone that was paid using the division's funds. The controller does not know I am aware of this information, or that I have a copy of his credit card statement. The person who provided me with the information works in the same division and cannot become known in this matter as the source of the information, nor can we acknowledge that we have a copy of the credit card statement. The controller will be able to identify who provided it to me immediately if it ever becomes known that we have it. The division has five employees at their location, and they manage their own finances. They collect their own revenues and pay their own bills. The controller keeps all the records for their division out at their location, and he has an office manager who helps keep things filed and organized. I need your help this weekend to think about what I just shared with you, and to come up with a plan to address this issue.

I want to deal with it as quickly as possible, and will be available all weekend if needed to react to this by Monday morning. What are your thoughts?''

FRAUD FACTS

Anonymous tips and complaints are the leading method of detection of fraud. According to the Association of Certified Fraud Examiners' 2008 Report to the Nation on Occupational Fraud & Abuse, tips accounted for 46 percent of all frauds detected, followed by 20 percent discovered by accident.[1] Tips included employee, customer, and vendor complaints, and were the leading detection method in their 2006 survey as well. The high percentage of detection by anonymous tips emphasizes an organization's need to educate employees regarding their fiduciary duty to provide information, as well as implement a means or process for individuals to provide such information. On the receiving end, the organization must implement a system to collect, screen, and process complaints and information when it is received.

I simply sat in the sun in silence, listening to Tim provide me with the details, and watching the sun set on my weekend plans. For an instant, I thought about how virtually every fraud embezzlement case had come to me on a Friday afternoon typically around 4:00, just in time to ruin a perfectly good weekend.

I told Tim I understood the gravity of the situation, and would be available to help him as much as needed throughout the weekend. I then started in with my standard host of questions, a process I call ''triage.''

I asked Tim these questions, and have included his responses.

''Other than the informant who provided the card statement, is there anyone else at the division aware that you know the controller may be stealing funds?'' Tim indicated he was certain the controller and the other staff did not know that the information was brought to his attention.

''Is there any reason to believe the controller knows his situation has been compromised, and would be destroying the evidence as we speak?'' Tim stated the informant called him to let him know the controller had left for the weekend as usual, and that nothing unusual or suspicious was noted with his behavior throughout the day. Tim indicated there would be no risk of loss of evidence by waiting and working on a plan over the weekend versus going to the division immediately and securing any evidence.

LEARNING POINT

Why would it be important to know if anyone was aware that the scheme had become known? Timing in these cases is everything. In virtually every fraud matter, the perpetrators maintained evidence of their crime, in the form of documents in a drawer, tracking the details in a notebook, or keeping files electronically on their computers. Once they feel their circumstance has been compromised by someone learning about their misdeeds, the evidence is almost immediately destroyed or removed offsite. If they have left the building for the day, they come back after-hours and steal or destroy the evidence. They also call co-workers and ask favors of them. Such favors could include deleting files and bringing physical files and information home with them. Fraud perpetrators have been known to break into their employer's buildings or even burn the building down in acts of desperation to ensure the evidence is never found and used against them. I had one case involving an employee embezzlement where the suspect burglarized the office, stole the receipts ledgers, and corrupted the computer files so no one could access the computerized accounting system the next morning. A week or so later the same office was burglarized a second time, only this time some of the accounting records were actually returned in a poor attempt to show they were there the entire time, buried below other papers and information. Desperate people do desperate things.

Knowing that, timing is of the essence in these cases. Typically, I like to deal with searching for evidence immediately after receiving a call such as Tim's. In my experience, too much happens if you wait until tomorrow morning. I drive right to their location regardless of the time of day, and secure any and all information possible, removing any possibility of it being lost, stolen, or destroyed. If I find any actual or potential evidence, it all leaves with me so I can be assured nothing will happen to it. If there are computers involved, they come with me as well.

"Do they have computers at their location, and are they backed up in a reliable fashion in the event the controller or anyone else potentially involved gets nervous and deletes the hard drives?" Tim indicated there were computers on each desk and a local area network, and that they performed their own backups on a regular basis. Tim was not aware of how the backup tapes were maintained.

"Is the organization's legal counsel involved and up to speed on this matter?" Tim stated he had been speaking with counsel throughout the week awaiting the credit card statement, and that as recent as late afternoon he had spoken to counsel about the status of the matter. Counsel was aware that Tim would be reaching out to me to solicit my involvement in resolving the matter.

LEARNING POINT

Why would you want to know about any computers, as well as if and how they were backed up? Just as with physical evidence, such as ledgers, checks, and bank statements, computer files and hard drives are at equal risk for corruption or deletion if not preserved in a timely fashion. Often, users have remote access into the business systems, and in some cases have access directly into their individual workstations, depending on the level of technology, sophistication, and authority involved. Once the computer hard drives have been deleted or physically stolen from the computers, recovering the files becomes much more difficult, if not impossible. Having reliable and secure backups of the drives creates a secondary plan in the event files are deleted or computer drives are deleted. However, if the backup tapes and drives are under the control of the same person or individuals potentially involved in the matter, both the computer drives and the backups are at risk of theft or destruction. Beating suspects to the punch by imaging the drives, making a backup, or taking possession of their computer will provide the best scenario for finding electronic evidence, if any exists.

Before setting out to preserve any potential electronic evidence, answers to a few questions may help. Are the computers desktops or laptops? Does the target use any other electronic devices, such as a hand-held phone or BlackBerry, to access his files and e-mails? The mobility of computers can create many issues and concerns—first and foremost, physically locating where the devices exist at any point in time. Chances are if the target uses anything but a desktop, his laptop and devices remain with him at all times. If the laptop is not at the organization, it will make it difficult to seize it or make an image of the hard drive without the user's knowledge.

Remote access to the organization's systems, files, and information may need to be disabled to the target once the investigation has been initiated. Knowing all the means the target has available to gain access will help ensure all points of access have been disabled, preventing the target from secretly accessing and deleting key files and information, or worse, stealing company information, such as client and customer lists or trade secrets, before being terminated.

FRAUD FACTS

The sophistication of an average perpetrator has likely been raised by what has been termed the *CSI* effect. In essence, individuals have been watching episodes of crime and forensic shows on television, and have learned what things are important in investigating various types of crimes. Much information is also available to a perpetrator through the Internet. One example is with software and technology available to remove files and evidence from computer hard drives. Wikipedia, the Internet-based encyclopedia, includes the term *anti-computer forensics*, which is defined as "a general term for a set of techniques used as countermeasures to forensic analysis." Much more information is included by Wikipedia in its definition, providing would-be perpetrators with knowledge that could aid them in preventing detection and recovery of supporting evidence.

LEARNING POINT

Legal counsel plays a very important role in every fraud investigation. First and foremost, no privilege exists between a client and an accountant, or a client and a fraud investigator. Any and all communications and procedures performed for the client will be wide open for discovery, and worse, the potential will exist that the very professionals retained to help the client resolve a matter could become witnesses against the client. To help ensure that all communications, procedures, and information are protected from discovery, the client should engage counsel to direct the inquiry or investigation. The accountant, fraud investigator, computer forensic specialist, and anyone else brought into the case should then be engaged directly by counsel. In order to preserve the privilege between the client and counsel, all communications should be directly to counsel, and all work performed should be clearly marked *confidential* and *attorney-client privileged*.

In many investigations, issues are identified within the victim organization beyond those relating to the fraud matter being investigated. In most cases, the discovered information could prove detrimental to the organization, and therefore may need to be protected by maintaining it as confidential. Having been engaged as a consulting expert directly by counsel will help preserve the information from being disclosed. Conversely, if counsel changes strategies later in the investigation and decides to disclose the same fraud professional as an "expert" for trial purposes, counsel does so at the risk that any and all information collected and discussed from the inception of the matter will be discoverable. This is something to keep in

(Continued)

mind and discuss with counsel before getting too far into the matter and preparing a well-documented file—potentially to be used against the client.

Second, issues will be encountered during an investigation, some more predictable than others, requiring legal advice. It is not uncommon for allegations to be raised by the target regarding the conduct of the victim organization. In searching for evidence you could encounter locked desks and cabinets within the control of targeted employees. Can you access the locked areas, or is there an expectation of privacy? The target may need to be placed on administrative leave. A whole host of legal issues may need to be contemplated, and having counsel engaged and available to provide direction and advice will preserve the integrity of the investigation.

"Is the human resource department involved in this matter at this point in time?" Tim indicated the human resource director was informed of the matter earlier in the day, and that she would be available as needed all weekend as well, to discuss how to deal with the matter.

LEARNING POINT

Equally important to counsel is the involvement of any human resources personnel within the victim organization. In smaller companies and organizations, no such resources typically exist, and a client would be wise to have counsel cover these areas of concern as well.

Targets of investigations should be subject to employment policies and procedures of the victim organization. Hopefully, formal documents in the form of employment handbooks exist and were issued to the employees, with signed acknowledgments obtained, evidencing the target's receipt of the policies. However, informal memos and e-mails may be the only form of documented policies in less sophisticated organizations. Employment policies often come into play in every investigation. Were employees put on notice that their e-mails, Internet activity, and all other electronic activity would be monitored and reviewed? What about defining appropriate versus inappropriate use of their computers? How about their phone usage and monitoring for personal use of company resources? Any mention of employees' expectation of privacy with their workspace areas? How about return of

(Continued)

(Continued)

company materials, property, computers, keys, and proprietary information upon termination of employment?

Targets of inquiries and fraud investigations are often placed on paid administrative leave pending the outcome of the investigation. This should be done to preserve both the integrity of the individual as well as the integrity of the investigation. Who will talk with the employee and place her on paid leave? How will the measure be documented in the employee's file? What happens when sufficient information and evidence is collected to terminate the individual's employment? Who is best to handle all aspects and requirements of termination, other than human resource personnel?

Most interesting is that many targets of a fraud investigation fire back allegations and counterclaims at the victim organization, forcing the organization to assume a defensive posture while on the offense of pursuing the original claim against the target. Claims of harassment, hostile workplace environment, and wrongful termination are common, regardless of the fact that the target may have stolen a significant amount of money from her employer. Individuals will also battle for unemployment benefits and funding of their retirement accounts even after admitting they stole money or assets from the organization. It is best to anticipate these issues and have the resources (counsel and human resources) on board as part of the investigative team to timely respond to any of these types of claims.

"What do you want to see happen, and on what timeframe are we dealing?" Tim stated he wanted first and foremost to ensure that any evidence supporting or negating the allegations is preserved, to minimize the need to solicit replacement information from third parties at the high costs banks and other financial institutions were charging. His timeframe was as soon as possible.

LEARNING POINT

Matters can be investigated in different ways, applying different strategies, and procedures can be modified and performed based on the desired goals or desired outcomes of the stakeholders, or victims. It is important to have an initial discussion at the onset of an investigation into a potential fraud matter identifying different investigative options. Criminal prosecution may be

(Continued)

desired from inception, or may be left for later discussions based on the evidence identified. Yet in other matters, criminal prosecution will be taken off the table and not desired. Restitution may be the biggest desired goal, but strategies and efforts to accomplish that goal may be hindered by the victim's desire to keep the matter out of the public eye. Access to information will become an issue as subpoenas and search warrants will not be options for collecting much-needed evidence. Knowing what the victim may be considering in the form of desired outcomes if in fact the fraud allegations are substantiated will help identify how the matter will be investigated, and the means and measures that will be available.

Equally important is managing a client's expectations. Fraud investigations take time, and educating a client up front that these matters are not resolved and adjudicated in weeks or months will help set the client's expectations from inception. Information requests could take weeks, and when received, often prove incomplete, leading to further subpoenas and court hearings. I always tell clients that a typical case could take three to six months to fully understand and investigate, and that no case is "typical."

The sense of urgency should be placed on two initial areas: preserving critical potential evidence and securing assets, bank accounts, investments, and other means for restitution. Once both of these areas have been addressed in a timely fashion, there is time to perform a thorough and objective investigation of the facts to form a conclusion based on the procedures performed and evidence collected.

• • •

I told Tim I would be available any time during the weekend, and thought it would be best to assemble a meeting with the executive director, human resource director, and outside counsel to discuss the matter and identify a strategy on how to resolve the allegations. Tim said he would call the other individuals and would target having a meeting Sunday afternoon, with the goal to identify a plan to be executed Monday morning. He thanked me for being available to support him on the matter.

I waited in anticipation for a call from Tim the rest of Friday night and Saturday morning, knowing he wasn't the type who was going to sleep or rest himself until the meeting was established and things were in motion.

Just before noon Saturday morning, as I packed our gloves, baseballs, and bats into my trunk to head to the park for some family baseball practice, my cell phone rang. I knew before I reached it that it was going to be Tim calling me. I was right. Tim indicated he had reached the others, and that with all their schedule conflicts throughout the weekend, the earliest we could meet was Monday morning at his office. I told Tim I would be there bright and early, ready to act as needed based on the outcome of the meeting. I told him to try to enjoy the rest of his weekend, knowing he probably wouldn't, and to call me anytime if anything changed.

THE IMPORTANCE OF PLANNING
(MAXIMIZING DESIRED OUTCOMES)

We were returning from dinner early Sunday evening when my cell phone rang. Since it was so late in the weekend and I hadn't heard from Tim since noon yesterday, I wasn't expecting it to be Tim calling me again. As soon as I looked at the number flashing on the display, I knew.

Tim apologized for calling, but wanted to let me know that the executive director would be unavailable to meet until tomorrow afternoon. Tim indicated all the other individuals could move the meeting into the afternoon, and now it was down to my schedule. I had already cleared the day and the following day knowing that, I would likely be out at the division at least one if not both days.

I told Tim the later time would be fine, and asked if anything new had been learned since yesterday's call. Tim said nothing new was identified but that counsel had been working with the human resource director reviewing the policies and employee handbook to prepare for the meeting. I was encouraged to know such documentation existed for this matter. I told Tim I would see him Monday afternoon at his office.

Monday morning's routine ran as usual. Up and showered, fed the kids breakfast, lunches packed, backpacks loaded, and off to their school we went. When I arrived at my office I called Tim to see if anything had changed, and to find out what time we were meeting. Tim indicated the meeting was at 2:00, and that if I wanted to get to his office earlier I could review the information and credit card statement prior to the meeting.

I focused on other client matters for the morning, and completed what I could knowing I would likely be consumed with Tim's matter for at least a few days during this week. I had a full schedule of meetings and client projects to address during the week, but as it happens when a new potential fraud case is identified, my schedule has to change to address the immediate concerns of the new fraud matter. After a few phone calls and e-mails, my schedule was cleared through Thursday.

It seemed like the morning dragged on forever, waiting in anticipation for the afternoon meeting. Finally at 12:00, I had reached my limit and headed out the door. I stopped at a sandwich shop on the way to Tim's office to ensure I had eaten before the meeting. Many previous times I skipped eating a meal only to have to perform immediate procedures, causing me to go without food for a long stretch of time. I have become more intuitive in my planning and bring snacks to ensure I get some form of nourishment in the event the meeting turns into a marathon day's worth of procedures ending late in the night.

● ● ●

I arrived at Tim's office, well fed and ready to get into the details. Tim was on the phone discussing late details with someone in preparation for the meeting. He motioned for me to sit in the chair in front of his desk, and he slid across to me a folder containing some documents. I put my briefcase down and sat as instructed, and reached for the folder.

Inside the folder was a copy of a United Alliance credit card statement. The card was in the target's name and included the mailing address of his division. The statement was limited to three pages in length, with individual charge transactions listed only on the first two pages. The third page was simply the reverse side of the second page and contained the small-font legal and account contact information found on the back of virtually every credit card statement. I scanned the charges and quickly noted that the charges were very likely personal in nature with no business purpose. The card account had a balance of about $23,000 at the beginning of the month. After one payment and many charges during the month, it had an ending unpaid balance of about $30,000. I noted the account had a significant balance, higher than most individual credit card owners' balances, but not even close to the much-higher dollar levels I had seen with other cases.

There was nothing further for me to look at. Three pages, and one was pretty much useless. I stared at the statement while waiting for Tim to complete his call, but nothing further came to me from my staring at the statement.

When Tim finished his call, we shook hands and he thanked me for coming over early to discuss the matter. He got up from his desk and walked over to close his office door. Then he returned to his desk, sat down, and reached for a folder from his lower desk drawer. Tim started flipping through the papers and began to tell me that he had dealt with this controller on other issues in the past. Tim indicated that their last issue involved the division's budget and their reporting, and Tim stated he thought the controller was not a credible individual.

Tim described the division and the four or five individuals who worked at the division. Tim stated the employees had been together for many years, and many if not all of the staff maintained a loyalty to their division's controller. Tim told me about the layout of their offices, and that they had desktop computers on each desk, networked together to form a peer-to-peer network environment. Tim also stated he believed the controller had a new laptop that he used as his workstation. Tim provided me with the names of the individuals working in the division, as well as a brief job description for each identified staff member.

It was amazing how quickly the time went by, and before I knew it we needed to head down to the conference room, as the others to be involved in this matter would likely be arriving. Sure enough, as we rounded the corner, the others were just getting to the conference room.

● ● ●

Everyone was present and accounted for at the table, with one surprise attendee added for good measure. Seated around the table were outside counsel, the executive director, the human resource director, Tim, myself, and a senior finance person who reported to Tim. Everyone looked to Tim to start the meeting.

Tim started out by reminding us that the matter about to be discussed was to be held absolutely private, and that everyone outside the assembled group with the exception of the informant had no knowledge about what was happening. Tim then scanned the table to ensure everyone acknowledged what he had said.

Tim distributed copies of the credit card statements to each person and allowed a minute or so to pass for review. Then he stated that he was unaware that the division even had a credit card. None of the other divisions had credit cards, and the only cards he was aware of were issued to and restricted to himself and the executive director. Tim stated that he retrieved and reviewed the detailed general ledger report for the division for the last fiscal year, and was unable to identify any payments being made to credit cards. Tim said he had had several private confidential conversations with the person who brought this credit card activity to his attention over the weekend, and the individual feared it would become known that they were the source of the investigation.

Tim shared with us that the individual still worked within the division, and was terrified of the controller and his office manager. Tim said that according to the informant, the controller had been skimming funds somehow through the division and funding a private bank account he had established at a bank separate from where the division maintained their accounts. Tim stated the individual believed the funds from that account were used to pay the credit card balance each month, and that the office manager was aware of the activity as he recorded all the activity for the division into the accounting system. Tim said the individual also stated the office manager received and reconciled the bank statements, and performed much of the other bookkeeping activity for the division at the direction of the controller. Tim ended by reminding us that how the information came to his attention would have to be crafted into a plausible story to avoid disclosing that an informant from the division provided the tip.

Ideas and suggestions were discussed around the table, and none of the stories seemed plausible. The credit card was in the name of the controller and included the division's mailing address. Any calls or mail from the card company would have been directed to the division, and we could not come up with a way to identify a link as to how *we* came upon the one-month statement in our possession. Then we started thinking of other storylines beyond the credit card statement. After much discussion, it was decided that we would go with a story involving the division's financial activities. We were instructed that if anyone asked how the matter was identified for investigation, we would indicate the information was confidential, and direct all inquires to Tim to handle. Otherwise none of us were to provide any response beyond sending the individual to speak with Tim. Tim and outside counsel arranged to discuss the story in further detail after the group meeting, to ensure what Tim provided was consistent with counsel's requirements.

LEARNING POINT

Specific laws exist to protect whistleblowers and confidential sources of tips, complaints, and information. One must be familiar with these laws and requirements, or run the risk of suffering unintended consequences that could cause more damage to the organization beyond the impact of the fraud itself being investigated. Retaliation lawsuits have had devastating financial impacts on organizations that failed to comply and protect the identity of individuals who brought matters to management's attention. Personal safety considerations are equally important for the confidential informant. Targeted individuals may lose their employment at the least, or be arrested and prosecuted at the most, based on information the informant provided to management. It is not uncommon for informants to fear physical harm through retaliation against themselves or their families. Death threats and harassment are not uncommon, and all efforts should be made to eliminate or at least minimize the risk of these consequences due to improper disclosure of the informant. In many cases in which I was personally involved, the true source of the information that initiated the investigation was never learned by the target or disclosed to anyone. It is amazing how many individuals have fallen victim to "random audits" of their financial accounts, only to have their fraudulent activity revealed through these random audits. In many cases, they are nothing but a ruse to protect how the information was actually learned.

With that completed, Tim turned his attention to me and asked me how we should proceed in investigating the provided information. Needless to say, I had many questions to be answered before I would propose a plan for the fraud investigation. Here are the questions I raised, along with the information I was provided.

"What will happen if we simply provided notice to the division that we would be conducting some internal audit procedures, and would be looking for financial information to be provided based on their records?" Tim immediately responded that it was likely the controller would realize something was up, as the organization had never completed anything even remotely close to any internal audit procedures. Tim continued by stating that the controller would likely ask for time to locate requested information, and would use that time to ensure any and all information pertaining to the potential fraudulent activity would be removed, destroyed, or deleted prior to our commencing of the procedures. Tim and the human resource director agreed that any advance notice provided to the controller or the office manager would likely tip them off, and any evidence in their possession would be gone.

As we discussed how we should approach the matter to collect evidence to minimize any notice to the controller and office manager, we identified that the best route to take to ensure evidence would not be destroyed or deleted would likely be accomplished through a surprise visit to the division on an unannounced, unplanned basis. I continued with my questions.

LEARNING POINT

There are pros and cons to performing unplanned, unannounced ("surprise") visits to locations. The benefits of this approach include catching individuals in the act and minimizing the risk that information that would have been available becomes missing or no longer found due to advance

(Continued)

notice provided, tipping off the potential targets. However, you would be reckless if you failed to consider the potential consequences of a "shock-and-awe" approach. Individuals beyond those involved in the potential fraud will be equally affected by the disruptions likely to occur due to your actions. Some individuals may become angry or supportive of the targeted individuals, while others may break down and become a resource drain requiring consoling. Often, phones will still need to be answered, transactions and activity will still need to be completed, and answers to questions will need to be provided—and there will be many individuals with many questions both within and external to the organization. Equal emphasis should be placed on potential consequences and solutions to those identified risks as on investigative issues.

"How many individuals work within the division?" The human resource director stated that six people, including the controller and office manager, worked in that location. She continued by telling us that the controller and officer manager were very close, and that they both work full-time mainly on weekdays. As for the other four employees, two worked full-time and two were part-time, and their schedules varied by position. I asked who was at the division today, and who would be there tomorrow if we needed to interact with them. The human resource director said the controller, office manager, and two others would be there today and tomorrow, and the others would be coming in later in the week as usual.

"Describe the controller and office manager, and tell me what their personalities are like." Tim indicated both individuals were quite difficult to work with and had attitudes. Tim stated the controller wasn't afraid to curse during heated discussions. Tim also said the office manager put on a front as being a tough guy, but in the absence of the controller, he is a pushover and utterly incompetent. The only reason he still had a job was because the controller liked him and kept him in that position, and that the controller has the authority to hire or fire his division's employees. Tim said he would love to see both terminated from the organization, and has for years. The human resource director concurred with Tim's description, and said if we could get the office manager away from the controller, he would cave in and give us anything we requested, unknowingly building a case against himself and the controller. She stated the source of his power and direction came from the controller.

Why would it be important to know what the individuals looked like and to solicit details regarding their personalities in advance? First of all, it would be good to recognize the individuals on the first visit to ensure you are talking with the correct individuals. Beyond identifying the right person, knowing as much as possible about any individual will prove extremely helpful when talking and dealing with him. If someone has a very hostile or angry demeanor, where and how you interact with him will likely be very different from where and how you interact with staff members who are very emotional. One interaction may be very private and need to be handled delicately to minimize the emotional breakdowns (crying), while the other may be best handled initially out in plain view with resources available in the event that the person becomes hostile toward you.

First and foremost, just as in working my weekend job driving ambulances, personal safety for yourself and the safety of all others involved in the investigation is the most important aspect to consider in any investigation. If there is any risk or potential risk that could jeopardize the safety of any individual, then a plan needs to be considered to ensure everyone's safety. No one needs to get injured or worse when investigating fraud matters. There are always multiple ways to accomplish measures and procedures, and if one could lead to a potential safety issue, then an alternative way needs to be identified and implemented to avoid the potential safety risk altogether. Ideally, if the investigation is planned properly with safety considerations discussed during the planning stage, anything that actually occurs involving safety concerns should have been contemplated and considered along with an identified plan to deal with each potential risk.

"Who has computers, and where are they located?" Once again the human resource director answered that she had been at the division recently to update personnel files. She remembered there were computers on each desk, with a laptop in use by the controller in his office. To the best of her memory, all the other computers were desktop computers with big monitors. She was unaware if the computers were connected to a centralized file server.

"Do we have a forensic computer specialist available to image and secure the electronic information, including images of each computer hard drive?" The group just looked at me, and their stares told me they had not considered that aspect of the investigation. I told them that I had a firm that I had used successfully on other matters and that with a phone call I could put them on notice that their assistance would be needed in this matter. Tim and outside counsel thought that it would be a good call to make, so I excused myself to the corner of the room and called the firm from my cell phone.

LEARNING POINT

Having technically competent resources available as part of the investigative team will maximize the effectiveness and thoroughness of any fraud investigation. Identifying professionals with experience and expertise within specific fields such as computer forensics will prove invaluable both during the investigation as well as during the resolution of the findings, including testifying at trial if needed. Electronically maintained information needs to be handled properly to ensure it is completely and accurately captured and stored. A simple mistake of booting a computer that was turned off could change files forever, as could shutting down a running computer. Experts who specialize in this field know best how to image drives and capture the information in a reliable and defendable manner, as well as how to recover deleted or hidden information once the systems have been properly imaged. Assembling a team of resources to call upon if needed is likely the best way to approach a fraud investigation. Finding the best specialists to use in each field is always the challenge.

I was successful in connecting with my contact, and quickly brought him up to speed. I asked him if they had capacity to react to this matter, and he indicated they were ready and available. I told him I would get right back to him once a plan had been identified. He said he would be waiting for my call.

I returned to the table and let the group know that the computer forensics firm was ready to go on my call.

"When do you want to make this happen, and who is available to accompany me on the visit?" I asked. Tim stated he wanted to execute a plan as quickly as possible, to minimize the risk that evidence would be deleted or destroyed if too much time passed. He added that he would be available to make the trip to the division accompanied by his senior finance person. The human resource director also stated she would be available to make the trip tomorrow to deal with any personnel issues on the spot, as they occurred. Outside counsel discussed the pros and cons of being on site during the visit and, after much discussion, decided it would be best to remain back at the office but available all day as needed by phone. A phone call would be all it would take to make the short drive to the division if it became necessary to have outside counsel on site. Everyone wrote down outside counsel's phone numbers to have with them, if needed.

The last to speak was the executive director. Acting as the voice of reason, he asked if it was absolutely necessary to barge into the division unannounced and commence performing procedures, and wanted to know if there was any other way this could be completed in a less disruptive manner. Tim first responded to the question and discussed again the risks posed if any notice was provided to the controller or office manager. Then, Tim discussed what procedures and costs would be involved if the controller and/or office manager were in fact committing a material fraud and destroyed all the evidence supporting their illegal activities. Once Tim finished, I corroborated what Tim said, and concurred that if the desired goal was to ensure any and all evidence was identified, controlled, and collected, then an unannounced visit was likely the only way to accomplish that goal.

Next, we discussed the logistics of executing an unannounced visit to the division. The controller and office manager knew Tim and the human resource director. If both of them showed up at the division and were spotted, evidence could be deleted or destroyed prior to gaining access to the individuals. Further, due to their personalities, it was likely that the controller would become a problem and a potential threat to safety in response to the unscheduled and sudden visit by "auditors," creating a scene in front of the other employees at a minimum and posing a potential safety concern to our team at worst. I indicated the best scenario would be to get the controller out of the office at the time of our arrival, leaving the office manager to fend for himself and deal with our unplanned arrival. That is when Tim came up with a brilliant suggestion. If the executive director called the controller in the morning to come to a meeting at the main office, the controller would likely comply and attend the meeting. If the executive director were to then call Tim on his cell phone to indicate the controller arrived at the main building, it would signal the team that it was clear to go to the division and interact directly with the office manager without interference from the controller. Only then, after the call was made, would the executive director inform the controller of the unplanned procedures being performed at his division.

• • •

All that was left to complete the meeting was to ensure we had the appropriate supplies and materials needed to execute the plan, and select a place and time to meet in the morning. I drafted a list of supplies to be obtained, and provided the list to Tim's senior financial person. Banker storage boxes, Sharpie markers, labels, legal pads, pens, garbage bags, and clipboards were needed, and lots of them. The human resource director would bring all the necessary forms and personnel files with her tomorrow should it become necessary to place any individuals on paid administrative leave.

Tim, the human resource director, and I would drive our vehicles to the neighborhood where the division was located for 12:00 the next day, then call each other to find a location in the area to meet and wait for the call from the executive director. The location would need to be close by but far enough away to not be seen from the division.

A plan was forged. We would arrive at the division once we received the signal, and take total control of the division location. Any individuals working at the division at the time of our arrival would be asked to come into the conference room, leaving their work areas immediately and in the exact condition as when we arrived. The human resource director and I would interview separately the office manager and any other employees on site, and have them identify where all financial information was maintained throughout their location. The office manager would then be placed on immediate paid administrative leave, and escorted out of the building without returning to his work area. Based on information provided during interviews of any other employees present, each would either be placed on paid administrative leave or at least be asked to leave for the remainder of the day, and return to work in the morning. Once the executive director informed the controller of the procedures being performed, the controller would also be placed on paid administrative leave and would not be permitted to return to the division's location.

Tim was to spend the rest of the afternoon identifying local resources in the area of the division, to be able to change locks on doors and reconfigure alarm system codes if needed after arriving at the division.

LEARNING POINT

We have a motto in emergency medicine when responding to calls. I am sure other fields use the same motto. "Plan for the worst, and hope for the best." It is always better to have contemplated all possibilities and have plans available, than to have to react unprepared. On most medical calls my crew brings all the resources into the house on a call, often knowing most of the stuff won't likely be needed. But every so often a call goes in a different direction than expected, and it is extremely fortunate that the very things we need are sitting right next to us in the house. Other crews have adopted a lesser standard, and every so often they get caught without needed equipment, delaying care to the patient.

In many cases, locks will need to be changed, access to the alarm systems and computer systems will need to be changed, and other physical safeguards will need to be implemented. Access to bank accounts and post office boxes will often need immediate changing as well. In order to preserve the integrity of the investigation as well as the business, these measures often need to be implemented immediately, leaving little time for planning. Knowing what resources are available in the geographical area will aid in soliciting the resources, as well as minimize the amount of time you need to spend at the site.

Tim also needed to draft letters to each of the banks that were known to have bank accounts in the name of the division, instructing each bank to freeze the activity within each account upon the delivery of the letter. The goal for tomorrow was to gain control of the division, and then lock down the bank accounts so that no further transactions could occur until further notice. Tim planned to leave the division once we arrived and things were under control, and deliver each letter to the banks to ensure the controller or office manager could not clear out any of the accounts.

LEARNING POINT

It is common for targets of investigations to access and/or withdraw funds from known and unknown bank accounts even after an investigation has been initiated. Monthly bank statements and other bank-provided information can also be redirected by an authorized signer on the account, preventing the investigator from gaining easy access to the statements and correspondence. Worse, though, is that once the target removes the funds from the account, it becomes a negotiation issue with the target, who is now holding the funds hostage, to get the funds returned. In the meantime, bills and payroll of the victim organization still need to be funded, and without access to the withdrawn funds, alternative means to maintain the organization's cash flow must be implemented.

The target's electronic access to banking and bank accounts must also be considered to ensure the target doesn't access the bank accounts after being removed from employment, even if only temporarily placed on paid leave.

Therefore, planning to take control over all known bank accounts, restricting who has access to the accounts, turning off any online access and telephone banking access, and providing new instructions to each bank identifying where bank statements and other bank information are to be mailed are all important measures to ensure the funds and reporting of the accounts remain intact.

I needed to call the computer forensics firm back and provide them with a brief version of the plan, so they could plan to be available at the site tomorrow once access had been gained. I knew I wasn't going to get a good night's sleep in anticipation of the unknown with tomorrow's plan.

COLLECTING THE EVIDENCE
(A.K.A. "THE RAID")

As predicted, I didn't get much sleep. Normal morning routine, and then I headed to my office to catch up on a few matters prior to driving out to the area of the division for 12:00. I couldn't wait in my office much longer, and headed out at 11:00. A bit early, but I knew I had to be out in the field waiting rather than sitting behind my desk. On my drive out, I called Tim to see if anything new had happened since we last talked at 5:00 P.M. yesterday. He indicated that he was heading out into the area as well, and we decided to meet at a local diner not far from the division to have an early lunch. Tim called his senior accountant, and before long the three of us were sitting in a booth rehashing the plan one last time over hamburgers and fries. Shortly after starting to eat our lunch, Tim's cell phone rang. The human resource director was calling to let him know she was in the area looking to meet up with the rest of the team. She indicated she was sitting in her car in a parking lot within view of the division, and that nothing unusual was happening.

We finished our lunch and headed back toward the division, looking for a place to sit and wait for the call from the executive director. Tim led the procession in his car, followed by me and the senior accountant. Tim pulled into a parking lot a few blocks from the division, and backed his car into a spot at the edge of the lot facing the business. I backed my car in next to Tim's, the senior accountant backed his car next in to mine, and the human resource director backed in last. Then, we rolled down our windows so that we could talk without getting out of our cars.

As we waited for the call, I noticed that the employees had gathered in the large window facing the parking lot, and were all staring at us. At that same moment, Tim's cell phone rang.

Tim answered his phone, and indicated to us it was the executive director calling to tell us the controller was with him, in his office. With that, Tim gave the thumbs-up sign and pulled his car out of the space. I followed Tim out of the parking lot, with the senior accountant and the human resource director directly behind me. As I looked back, I watched the employees follow our four cars with their stares as we left their lot. A big sigh of relief for them, I am sure.

I followed Tim to the small parking lot next to the building, while the senior accountant and human resource director parked in front of the building. Tim and I walked around the side and met up with the others and we walked to the front door as a group. Tim took the lead and opened the front door to their building, and was greeted immediately by the office manager. Tim identified himself as the chief financial officer of the organization, and stated to the office manager that we were there to perform an audit of the financial records. With that, Tim pushed on through the door toward the office areas, followed closely by the office manager. I watched the office manager to ensure he didn't take or touch anything, and as we entered the offices I noticed a woman working at a desk, with a "deer in headlights" look on her face.

I instructed the office manager to head directly into the conference room without going to his work area or touching anything, and the human resource director asked the woman working at her desk to get up and follow us into the conference room. Both followed without touching anything and I stayed with them in the conference room with the human resource director while Tim and the senior accountant walked through the division looking for other employees. They returned a moment later and indicated there was no one else in the building.

LEARNING POINT

Keeping control over the scene and situation is key to maintaining safety issues as well as preserving evidence. I have heard many stories from victims and colleagues who have investigated financial issues where the target was allowed to return to his work area, or worse, asked to come to a meeting at

(Continued)

his convenience, only to use that opportunity to delete files, change passwords, destroy evidence, and eliminate any and all information within his control so it could not be used against him. If a decision has been made that evidence could exist and the target does not know his potential scheme has been illuminated, the best possible scenario is to immediately separate the target from the areas where evidence may exist. If his computer is on, leave it where it is and in the condition it was found. If it is off, leave it off. Secure it.

The senior accountant took the woman into a small office while I remained in the conference room with the office manager and human resource director. I identified myself to the office manager, and indicated to him that we needed to ask him some questions regarding his role and responsibilities within the division. The office manager agreed to talk with us, although still quite shocked by our abrupt appearance at his location. Before I asked my first question, he asked us where the controller was and why we were doing an audit while the controller was out of the office. I stated that the controller was not informed of the audit until this morning, and that the information we sought would not necessarily need his involvement. Just then, the office manager's cell phone rang. As he looked down to see who was calling, I looked at the human resource director and nodded. The office manager answered the call and indicated to the caller that we had just arrived and were starting to ask him questions about his job and the finances. I could hear the caller across the table, and he ended the call by stating he would be at the division shortly. The human resource director also heard the caller, and left the room to let Tim know that the controller would be coming to the division shortly.

As soon as he ended the call, I asked him basic background questions (What is your name, How long have you worked here, What is your position, Do you have a title, etc.). He provided responses to all of my questions. I asked him where the accounting system was located and on which computers the files resided. He stated the accounting system and all the files for the division resided on his hard drive, and that through a peer-to-peer network he had configured in the office, the controller and the woman with the "deer in headlights" expression could access the files from his hard drive using their separate computers.

I asked him where all the computers were located. He identified four desktop computers, as well as a new laptop used by the controller. I asked him where the controller kept his laptop. He indicated it should be on the center of his desk. I asked him where the financial files and records were stored within the division. He stated the files were stored in multiple locations throughout the building, with the most recent files maintained in drawers in and behind his desk. He also stated the most current bills and deposits were in a bin on top of his desk. I asked him if he would be willing to show me where the financial files and computers were located, and he agreed to show us the locations.

I asked him to identify all of the banks and bank accounts utilized by the division. He named various banks and accounts, and I listed the accounts in my notebook. I asked him if there were any other bank accounts and he stated there were none. I asked him if the division used any credit cards and he stated there were none. I asked him who generated all the checks and signed the checks, and he stated that he generated all the checks, but that the controller signed all the checks. He also said the controller maintained his own set of records over certain accounts and therefore had little to do with those accounts. When I asked him to identify what accounts he was referring to, he said we should ask the controller himself about those accounts. He provided no further details about the accounts.

We left the conference room and the three of us walked throughout the building. As he identified the various locations, I asked him what information was stored in each area. I carried my steno pad and made notes of each location along with the described contents provided by the office manager. He identified files maintained in multiple locations throughout the building and showed us the five computers (four desktops plus one laptop). He stated that two of the computers were old and no longer used. He showed us the newer laptop that was actually sitting on the controller's desk (another sign that they had no idea this was about to happen).

Once he identified the last location and indicated there were no further records or computers in the building, we returned to the conference room. I asked him if he had any files, records, or other information pertaining to the division at his house or any other location outside of the building, and he indicated he had no other records pertaining to the division. I asked him for any passwords that we would need to access the systems and programs. He provided me with the network system administrator password, and said that if I logged into the network using the Admin user ID and password, I could change any of the users' passwords. Therefore he would not provide his personal password. I asked him if QuickBooks had any passwords, and he provided me with the password to access QuickBooks. I made sure I documented all the user IDs and passwords he provided in my notebook for future use. With that I thanked him for his time and cooperation and left him in the conference room with the human resource director.

After I left the conference room, the human resource director indicated to the office manager that he was being placed on paid administrative leave and that he would be escorted back to his desk to retrieve his jacket and would be escorted out of the building. He was provided with some forms, escorted to his desk by the human resource director and Tim, and then walked out the front door. I watched as he was walked out. He was not happy, but got into his car and drove away. I watched out the window to ensure that he actually drove away and did not return to the building.

LEARNING POINT

As discussed earlier, safety should always be a concern when doing fraud investigations. Placing an individual on administrative leave, or worse, terminating an individual's employment, could present a potential risk to those involved, due to the unknown of how the individual will react. Being prepared, having a plan, and identifying potential risks regarding the individual will help the situation. Until the individual leaves the property, there may be a safety risk to those involved, as well as to others like co-workers, supervisors, and management. Observing individuals until they leave the property will identify if they potentially retrieve a weapon from their vehicle and return toward the building. It is unfortunate that such measures need to be contemplated, but in today's society, such events are not uncommon, and preventing yourself from being "surprised" should always be a concern.

I went to the office with the senior accountant and the woman who had been working at her desk across from the office manager's desk when we first arrived. I asked her similar basic background questions, and shared with her the information regarding the computer and financial records locations identified by the office manager. I asked her if there were any other computers or locations for storing financial records that were not identified by the office manager. She reviewed my notes and stated that she did not know of any other computers or locations. She also stated her job did not involve accessing or maintaining financial records, and that she would not know all the areas that the records were stored. I left the woman in the office with the human resource director, and I returned to the office area along with the senior accountant.

• • •

Tim was busy on his cell phone talking with the executive director about his interaction with the controller. When Tim completed his call, he indicated that the controller had become very angry and stormed out of the office. Tim stated that based on the timing, the controller would be arriving at the division any minute, and that he should be solely responsible for dealing with the controller when he arrived.

I walked the building with the senior accountant and made more notes describing each office and room along with a brief description of the contents in each area. I made notes of every computer identified in the building along with the specific location and the current state of each computer (turned on or off, screen locked or opened, application on the screen if still running . . .). Once completed, I called the computer forensic specialists from my cell phone to let them know we had taken control of the division and that they needed to come and collect the computers for examination. I provided them a brief description of each computer to ensure they came with the appropriate equipment, and asked them to come to the front door when they arrived.

As I ended the call I saw a man coming toward the front door. I found Tim and let him know that someone, likely the controller, was heading toward the front door. Tim moved toward the front door, and as the door opened, Tim was standing right there to intercept him. It was in fact the controller and he was pretty angry. Tim brought the controller into a private office and met with him for quite a while, and I later learned that Tim also had the executive director on his cell phone during their conversation.

I instructed the senior accountant to retrieve the supplies from his car so that we could start systematically going through all the areas of the division, collecting the evidence that needed to be preserved. While the senior accountant was gone, I retrieved my digital camera and took some pictures of the different offices and areas while no one was around. I took pictures of each area where financial records were identified as being stored by the office manager and I took pictures of every computer, including what was on each monitor.

The senior accountant returned with a stack of banker boxes and Sharpie markers, and I looked around quickly to determine an efficient and systematic means to search each area. We identified a box-numbering scheme, and I asked the senior accountant to record the box number and the location within the building as the contents were collected. I also asked him not to mix items from different areas and to use a separate box for each distinct area. With that, we both started to assemble banker boxes and marked the boxes in numerical order.

LEARNING POINT

You need to be prepared. Collecting evidence in fraud-related cases tends to be voluminous. Having the supplies on hand will prove invaluable as the information is identified, collected, and preserved. Beyond the boxes and labels needed, you need to consider how all those boxes and computers will be transported to a secure location. A small car with 20 or more boxes will become an issue. Equally important is being organized in the collection process. Numbering and labeling will help, but you will also want to keep track of where each box's contents were collected. These things will all need to be documented in your notebook, but why not make your life easier by documenting that information right on the boxes themselves.

The human resource director came out of the office with the woman, and watched her as she collected her pocketbook and keys from her desk. Then, she escorted her out the front door and watched as she got into her car and drove away. She then came and joined us in the office area. She said the woman was very upset by what had happened this afternoon, and although she didn't believe she was involved in the finances of the division, thought it would be best to send her home for the rest of the day. She said once the woman regained her composure, she asked if she could collect her things and leave. She said the woman stated she would be willing to talk with us, but just not this afternoon.

Having no one else to interview or send home, the human resource director asked me how she could help us with our search. I provided her with an empty box and marker, explained to her the numbering scheme and location notation for the boxes, and placed her in one of the offices to go through all the areas looking for any financial records.

I let the senior accountant start in the area of the office manager's desk. I started with the office immediately adjacent to the business office. I began by drawing a rough sketch of the office, a floor plan, and once documented I started on my left and worked clockwise around the entire office. I opened every drawer, looked at everything kept on every shelf, and went through the entire desk in the office. I retrieved a garbage bag from my case, emptied the garbage can contents into the bag, and sealed the bag. Then I wrote out a tag identifying the location of the contents within the garbage bag. I found financial documents and records in several areas in the office. I collected the information and placed it into banker boxes labeled for that office. Records included bank statements, deposit details, and payroll records.

As I searched the office, I took breaks to check on how the senior accountant and the human resource director were making out with their areas. Each had made some progress and filled several boxes, but based on that progress, I knew we would be at the division for quite some time. I collected more empty boxes for my area and continued searching to complete the area.

• • •

A short while later I noticed another individual out on the sidewalk heading toward the front door. I recognized him as the computer forensic specialist I had called. He was someone that I had worked with several times on prior matters. I greeted him as he arrived at the front door and brought him into the office area. Once I introduced him to the others, I brought him through the building and identified all the computers identified to me by the office manager. He took out his pad and made notes for each computer, and also took pictures of each computer. Once I had shown him all the computers, I left him to do what he needed to do and returned to the office that I was searching.

Once I finished collecting everything from the office I was searching, I returned to the business office area to help the senior accountant complete that area. By far, the office manager's area contained the most financial information, at least for the current and previous year. The remaining historical information was stored in boxes in another area of the building. I would guess it took the two of us a good hour or more together before we completed the office manager's area.

Tim reappeared from his closed-door meeting and informed us that the controller was in the process of collecting his personal belongings and would be leaving the building shortly. Tim, then, returned to the office where he met with the controller, and a short time later both of them emerged from the office. Tim escorted the controller out the door and we watched as he loaded his things into his car and drove away. A big sigh of relief could be heard from all the team members once he had left the building.

Tim then started calling the locksmith and alarm company from his cell phone to have them come and make the changes we had already anticipated making.

LEARNING POINT

As part of planning, you should have already identified locksmiths in the area, as well as whether they perform service on a 24-hour basis. Locks will need to be changed on the spot before the scene will be considered secured from unauthorized access by the target. Whether an alarm system is involved should also be determined in advance, and the contact information for the alarm system should be identified, if possible, in advance. I don't believe either should be provided advance notice, as either could have a relationship with the target, providing a means for the target to be tipped off about the imminent investigative measures to be executed.

I left the office areas to be completed by the senior accountant and human resource director and headed into another area of the building with boxes and markers. I noticed two black file cabinets on my journey through the building that had not been described by the office manager. I opened the cabinets and found historical financial records for the division, albeit older than likely needed. I documented the file cabinets' location and contents within my notepad, and considered the need to collect the older information. I decided the information was likely too old and not relevant, so I retrieved my bag and took out a roll of evidence tape. I unrolled the tape and placed a seal across the front of all the drawers in the file cabinets to ensure no one went into the file cabinets. Later I would learn that I left that roll of tape on the file cabinets and would have to buy a new one for future investigations.

I reached my planned destination area of the building and found financial records and reports, paid invoices, and other records from earlier fiscal years. The records pertained to periods two or more years ago, but because we had no idea how long the potential scheme could have been occurring, I decided all the records would need to be collected and preserved. I started making more banker boxes, placing the records into the boxes, and labeling the boxes. I finished the area some ten boxes later, and looked around to ensure I had not missed any records. I was also out of boxes.

• • •

I met up with the computer forensic specialist who was collecting the computers throughout the building and bringing all of them to one table near the front door. I could see on his pad that he had sketched the area of each computer, as well as made notes for each computer. Once he brought the last computer to the front, he asked me if he could take possession of the laptop sitting on the controller's desk. I found it interesting that the controller went to his desk to retrieve his personal items and left the laptop on his desk behind when he left the building.

We went and found Tim and the human resource director talking in a hallway. We asked them about the controller's laptop left on his desk. We indicated the laptop was closed and appeared to be shut off. Tim indicated that the informant had mentioned the controller's laptop, and thought the controller had purchased it recently with his own funds. That being said, the question was whether it was the property of the organization or the controller. If it was the organization's, then seizing and examining the laptop drive contents would not be an issue. However, if it turned out to be the controller's personal laptop, then we would need to think through whether we should access the laptop drive without the controller's knowledge and consent. The human resource director knew nothing about the laptop to provide any guidance regarding the organization's technology policies.

The fact that the controller removed his personal belongings in the presence of Tim, and left the laptop behind on his desk, raised some interesting questions. Was the controller relinquishing his ownership of the laptop by leaving it behind, or could the controller have left it behind as a trap for the investigation? In order to ensure we did not jeopardize the entire investigation, we contacted counsel.

LEARNING POINT

It is for exactly such issues as the laptop that it is best to have counsel on board and available to provide guidance. If we were to seize and access the laptop, only to learn it was the personal property of the controller, our actions could undermine all the other well-contemplated measures and procedures in the case. If by chance there was a "smoking gun" in the case and it resided on the laptop, our access could prove detrimental to the entire case if it later was successfully argued that we should not have accessed the laptop in the first place. A better route would be to secure the laptop, seal it, and wait for legal guidance on a decision as to whether it can be accessed or imaged.

It was a good time to utilize counsel's advice for the laptop issue as well as the controller's office in general. No one had surveyed the office since the controller left the building, and it needed to be searched for any financial records. However, given the fact that the controller locked his office at night, there was a chance the controller had created some level of privacy. As with the laptop, advice on where we could search and what we could collect as potential evidence would be needed to ensure the investigation was conducted properly.

Tim called counsel using his cell phone, and once connected, put counsel on speakerphone. Tim, the human resource director, the computer forensic specialist, and I were all in the controller's office. Tim explained that the controller had left the building after collecting his personal belongings from his office, and left a laptop on the center of his desk. Tim asked if we were authorized to seize the laptop as evidence and allow the computer forensic specialist to image the hard drive. Counsel asked how the laptop was acquired. Tim indicated he thought the organization purchased it, but that the informant had told him he thought the controller purchased it personally. Counsel asked several more questions, and once answers were provided, counsel made a determination that we should seize and secure the laptop for the time being, but that we should hold off from accessing or imaging the hard drive until further research could be performed to determine if the organization had in fact purchased the laptop.

The computer forensic specialist drew a sketch of the laptop and location in his notebook, and then took several pictures of the laptop in its original location. Then I put an evidence seal over the opening edge of the laptop and a second one across the hard drive cover plate, to prevent anyone from opening the laptop or removing the hard drive. I then made notations in my notebook, and turned the laptop over to the senior accountant, who placed the laptop into a numbered banker box. The box was placed with all the other boxes of potential evidence collected up to that point, and a real pile of boxes was accumulating.

● ● ●

We turned our attention to the controller's office. Counsel remained on speakerphone as we described the different areas of his office. His desk was centrally located with seven drawers, three on each side and one in the center. None of the drawers were locked. There was a stack of papers and information on the top-left surface of the desk, along with other stacks on shelves on the wall. As we described each area, counsel provided permission to access the area and search for any financial information. There was a trash bin on the floor to the left of the desk, and the bin was full of discarded papers. Counsel allowed us to collect the contents in the trash as the controller had placed the information in the trash, eliminating any expectation of privacy.

I was responsible for the controller's desk along with the trash bin. Tim and the human resource director worked the shelves along the wall, and the senior accountant worked within both areas by providing boxes and documenting the areas to ensure the seized information did not get co-mingled. As I went through each drawer I found nothing regarding financial matters. The trash bin, however, contained discarded envelopes, some of which included the names and logos of credit card companies. Envelopes were found, but no statements or information regarding the actual credit card accounts. Still, the envelopes told us that credit cards did in fact exist, something we could now use to connect our procedures to our knowledge that credit cards likely existed. I bagged the trash bin contents in their entirety, and labeled and numbered the garbage bag.

Invoices and statements for what appeared to be personal expenditures were found in the stack on the controller's desk, as well as within the stacks on the shelves. The invoices included cellular phone bills, insurance policies, and other non-organizational expenses. I showed Tim the insurance invoice for short-term disability coverage. The invoice listed the controller and office manager as well as the controller's father, an individual not even employed by the organization. Similar coverage was found in the invoices for health and dental coverage. The controller's father's insurance coverage was included within the division's policies and premiums, and there were notations that the father's premiums were being paid for, or reimbursed by, the controller or his father. That notwithstanding, the father should not have even been on the organization's policies as he was not an employee. Now we knew the potential problem was likely bigger than the reported skimming and personal use of credit cards. It appeared the division was using organizational funds for personal, unauthorized purposes.

As we were finishing the controller's office, there was a knock on the front door at the main entrance. Tim left to determine who was at the door. I walked over and watched through the window in the office. Tim answered the door and let a gentleman in. Tim looked over and said it was the locksmith. He showed the locksmith the front doors and then brought him through the location, identifying other doors with locks that needed to be changed. Tim asked the locksmith to change all the locks that provided access to the building, and also asked that all the locks be keyed the same to streamline and simplify controls over the keys. Under the existing lock configuration, a different key was needed for every point of access. The locksmith indicated changing the locks and using one common key would not be an issue. He also stated it would take an hour or two, but that he could have all the locks changed today. This was good news, especially for Tim and me, in that no unauthorized access to the building would be gained once we left, but more importantly, we would not have to spend the night in the building to ensure no one accessed the building until the locks were changed.

Within minutes of the locksmith's arrival there was another pair of workers walking up the front walk toward the building. Tim saw them from the window, looked over at me, and said it was the alarm guys. Tim met the pair at the door, and looked back at me while nodding. It was the alarm guys he called to disable the old alarm codes and add new access codes to the system. Tim led the workers to the alarm system access panel, and left them alone to determine the system requirements.

● ● ●

I returned to the business office area and helped the senior accountant complete the area. The senior accountant had completed the office manager's desk as well as the trash bin alongside his desk. As I walked into the room the senior accountant waved me over and pointed to some papers on the top of the office manager's desk. I asked the senior accountant where he found the papers he had placed on the desk, and he indicated he had found them in the trash bin. I flipped through the few papers, and the most interesting paper was a new-account-opening confirmation with a bank located just down the street. The new-account confirmation was dated four days earlier, and I immediately remembered asking the office manager if there were any new bank accounts and his response that there were none. Then we find a new-account confirmation in his trash bin dated four days earlier. Two issues came to mind regarding the found account information. First: The office manager clearly lied about not having any other accounts, but why? Second: Why was a new account opened four days earlier, when clearly the controller and office manager had no idea we would be coming to the division to perform a surprise audit?

LEARNING POINT

When searching for evidence, you need to consider all the areas where evidence could be found, including trash bins, recycling bins, shredders, and dumpsters. In my experience, significant evidence supporting allegations has been found in these areas, as was the case in this matter. While cross-cut shredders would prove to be a challenge for reconstructing shredded documents, the ribbon-cut shredder allows a much easier piecing together of the shredded documents. The large, often blue-colored shredding boxes found throughout larger organizations don't require any reconstruction at all, as the documents are slipped into these collection bins intact for future shredding. Collect everything possible, because if it is not collected it could be lost forever. You can always sort it out later and discard what is not needed.

We spent the entire day at the division collecting and preserving potential evidence while the locksmith changed the locks and the alarm guys modified the alarm system along with new access codes. As areas were cleared, the boxes were brought up to the business office area. The boxes were placed in numerical order, and I wrote out a listing of the boxes in my notebook. A total of 26 boxes, four computers, and four garbage bags were collected and listed.

Once completed, the computer forensic specialist carried one of the computers out to his car. It was still light outside, and he parked out front to shorten the walk from the building. I followed with the second computer, and we both made a second trip to bring out the remaining two computers. I noted in my notebook the time the computers were turned over to the computer forensic specialist, and indicated to him that I would call in the morning to see how the imaging went. I stood out front and watched him drive away for the night.

● ● ●

When I walked through the front door I noticed the locksmith had put away his tools and was talking with Tim. Moments later they shook hands and the locksmith went out the front door, leaving Tim with a few shiny new keys. Tim walked over and tried each key in the front door, to ensure each worked before the locksmith left. Tim then handed one key to the human resource director, and placed the remaining keys in his pocket. I asked Tim where we were going to store the boxes and bags for the night to ensure control was maintained for chain-of-custody purposes. I indicated we could transport all the boxes and bags to my office where they would be stored within the secured evidence room. However, access to the boxes and bags would be restricted unless I was there and available to provide access. Tim thought of alternative locations, and identified a private storage room within the main office. Tim indicated the storage room was locked, and that access was limited to certain designated individuals. Tim said he would secure the room for the night, and have the lock changed in the morning so that he had the only key to access the room. Tim also stated that due to the lateness of the hour, no other individuals with potential access would still be in the building, and he could control access until such time as the locks were changed. It was agreed that all the boxes and bags would be transported directly from the division to the main office, and secured in the locked storage room for the evening.

As I discussed with the senior accountant and human resource director how we were going to get all the boxes and bags back to the main office, Tim went to check on the status of the alarm system guys. Tim returned and indicated they would be finished within a few minutes, and that they would need to show him and the human resource director how to arm and disarm the system.

I decided we should move the boxes and bags from the building through the side entrance to minimize the risk that our stream of boxes leaving the building could bring unwanted attention to our mission. I walked down to the side entrance and looked out to see if there was room to move other vehicles to the side of the building. I asked the senior accountant to move his car around the side, and started moving boxes from the business office closer to the side door entrance. I started carrying boxes in numerical order out to my car, as did the senior accountant. Tim and the human resource director joined us once the alarm system guys had left the building, and together we filled three cars with all the boxes and bags.

LEARNING POINT

Every detail should be contemplated when possible in order to ensure the goals or desires of the engagement are accomplished. In this case no media or outside attention was wanted, and the goal was to be as discreet as possible.

(Continued)

Leaving with the boxes out the front door to waiting cars would have likely drawn attention to what we were doing. By using the side access, our cars were hidden by the garage from the busy street out in front. While a street ran alongside the building, there was much less auto and pedestrian traffic on that side, minimizing our exposure. Staging all the boxes near the exit of the building also allowed the quickest and most efficient means to fill the cars, minimizing the amount of time we could have been seen by anyone else.

I updated my notebook with the time we completed the procedures at the division as well as the box numbers within each car. I also documented who accompanied each set of boxes and bags on their journey from the division back to the main office. Tim, the senior accountant, and I sat and waited in our cars as the human resource director shut off the lights, closed up the building, set the alarm, and locked the side door after she exited the building. I noted the time the building was locked.

The human resource director thanked us for a job well done, got into her car, and drove off for the evening. Tim pulled out next, followed by the senior accountant and myself. We drove directly from the division to the main office. When we arrived a short time later, Tim went in to open up the building, while the senior accountant and I remained in the parking lot with the cars.

LEARNING POINT

In order to ensure the collected evidence can be presented in a case and survive scrutiny regarding the collection, handling, and maintenance of each item, each item of evidence must be properly collected, marked, tracked, and secured from the time each item is located up through the time each item is presented in court. Each item must also be preserved in the exact state and condition in which it was found.

The controlling and tracking of each evidence item from start to finish is known as preserving the chain of custody. Any potential break in the chain could lead to the evidence being ruled inadmissible, and many well-known highly publicized cases have been ruled on based on the admissibility or inadmissibility of evidence. If a piece of evidence was the "key piece," or

(Continued)

(*Continued*)

it was critical to proving or disproving the case, the entire outcome of the case could be forever changed, likely to the detriment of the party who sought to present the evidence.

Therefore, thought and consideration must be directed toward how evidence will be collected, recorded, tracked, and maintained. This could be as simple as collecting a signature stamp used by an employee for processing unauthorized check disbursements, or as complex as dealing with a warehouse full of documents, ledgers, statements, and other financial information. Collection, transporting, tracking, and maintenance will be distinctly different based on the two extremes. The mechanics of how this would occur will also vary greatly based on what is available and being provided.

The information to be sought as potential evidence could be in paper form, or it could be stored electronically as files. For electronically stored information, it could be on site on a hard drive of a local personal computer, or it could be maintained on a virtual file server located anywhere on the Internet. How access will be gained, how it will be authenticated and preserved, and how it will be maintained will all be dependent on the location and volume of the electronic data.

Tim exited the building through a door in the rear, and walked over to retrieve his car. We drove closer to the open door and parked. We carried the boxes and bags one by one to the doorway. Each box was brought directly into the designated storage room, and when the last box was placed in the room, I inventoried all the boxes and bags to ensure they were all included and properly stored. I updated my notebook describing the transport and storage, and noted the time. I then placed a small piece of evidence tape across the door to the frame to ensure no one accessed the room until I returned in the morning. Then Tim locked the door and shut the lights in the hallway. The senior accountant and I waited out in the dark by our cars as Tim locked up the building.

When Tim came around we talked in the dark about the day's events. Tim thanked us for our efforts, and stated he was pleased that the planned measures went off without a hitch. Tim expressed his surprise that no media had been tipped off once we arrived and took control, and was pleasantly surprised that it seemed no one even noticed us carrying computers and all the boxes and bags from the building into our vehicles. Given the busy area in which the division was located, it was contemplated that such things could have occurred. Therefore, these issues were identified during the planning stages, and measures were identified to respond to the issues including directing all questions to Tim in the event of media or any other parties appearing and asking questions.

LEARNING POINT

Proper planning contemplates as many potential risks and issues as possible, as well as identifies steps and measures to be taken should each risk or issue materialize. It is always the hope that as few measures as possible will actually be needed.

In this case the media could have been tipped off by any of the individuals who were removed from the building, or someone could have simply spotted the computers and boxes being carried out from the building if they happened to be passing by in the area. It would not be a stretch for an alert or nosy neighbor or passerby watching the activities to contact the media or the police, resulting in unwanted attention on the situation.

Preserving the integrity of any parties and the investigation should be of paramount concern, and little to no information should be provided unless the information to be provided has been planned and approved by the organization and counsel.

Identifying who should handle the media and what every other individual involved should say or do are important issues to discuss and plan prior to initiating an investigation. Preparing a statement or response for the identified point person to provide to the media should the media become aware of an investigation is also important.

While these are important aspects to consider in an investigation, they are often ignored or overlooked risks or issues in many investigations. This is clearly evident by the surprised and unprepared look and response of an unsuspecting individual captured by a looming camera crew and reporter at a scene.

Equally important is the consideration of a prepared statement or response when news of an investigation, or the results of an investigation, could become public information. Many times the nature and tone of the media story can be directly influenced by voluntarily releasing facts and information to the media, which could result in a much better story for the organization.

It was late and time to head home. Tim said he would be in first thing in the morning when the building opened at 8:00. I asked him not to access the storage room until I arrived. I wanted to be able to document that I cut the evidence tape over the door, breaking the seal, to ensure that no one had accessed the room during the night. Due to my morning family obligations, we agreed to meet at 8:30.

CHAPTER 4

REVIEWING THE EVIDENCE
(THE DAY AFTER)

That night I had a late supper and tried to unwind as I spent time with my family. The day was fresh in my mind, and I knew that once they went to bed I would have more time to work on the case. Many things happened during the day's events, and I have learned it is best to capture as many details as possible while they are still fresh in my mind.

I found my notebook from the day. I also retrieved my Dictaphone, a mini–voice recorder I used to capture information for memos and documents. Flipping through my notes, starting from the beginning of the notebook, I recorded the day's events as best I could recall using my notes and my memory (albeit a very tired memory). I was able to dictate two complete tapes, both sides, before completely running out of energy (about 60 minutes' worth of information).

The morning came amazingly fast, and I knew I wanted to get to my office to drop off the tapes with my administrative assistant so that she could type them into memos the same day. As I planned my day, I realized that there was no way I was going to be at the building by 8:30 after dropping off the tapes unless I managed to get the morning routine accelerated a bit. I completed the morning drop-off at school earlier than usual, and then ran to my office. As luck would have it, I hadn't thought about needing my laptop, but seeing it on my desk reminded me to bring it along. I was back on the road in a flash, and was pleasantly surprised when the traffic was lighter than usual. I pulled into the parking lot with five minutes to spare.

As I went to the trunk to retrieve my laptop, I grabbed a note-book, a new tape for my Dictaphone, and a box of permanent markers. Although collecting all the boxes and bags of potential evidence yesterday was exciting, I was now dreading having to look through 26 boxes and 4 bags of information.

LEARNING POINT

A key to a successful investigation is the ability to maintain complete and accurate detailed notes. It would be best to record them along the way as things occur, rather than relying on your memory to recollect the details and documents at a later date. While writing in a notebook would be an efficient means, there may be other ways to memorialize the details as they occur, and later have them put into a more permanent format, such as your notebook. Having a pocket dictating device, whether digital or tape, could prove invaluable when you need to capture details but can't write them down in your notebook. An advantage to using electronic recordings is that it allows you to record as it occurs, and also allows you to capture details while doing other things, such as driving back at night from a meeting. The taped notes can be transcribed later into your written notes without losing the rich details. As a rule of thumb, I try and capture sufficient details to allow me to recollect what happened, when, where, and why, three years from when the notes were taken. It is not uncommon for a case, especially the civil aspects of a matter, to be heard and resolved two to three years or more down the road.

• • •

I met Tim in his office, and we walked down the hall to retrieve the senior accountant. Tim indicated that the senior accountant would be working with me to go through the boxes and bags. We walked to the storage room, and the tape was still intact as we left it last evening. I noted the date and time in my notebook, and then cut the evidence tape to allow Tim to open the door. As the door opened and he flicked on the lights, I noticed the rather large collection of boxes, and could only imagine how long it would take to go through the contents of each and every box and bag.

Tim had reserved a large meeting room right around the corner from the storage room, and told us both rooms would be available as long as needed to complete the investigation. One by one we carried the boxes and bags from the storage room into the meeting room and placed the boxes and bags on the floor in numerical order. After several trips, all of the boxes and bags were lined up on the floor of the meeting room. Tim left us to begin the task of inventorying and documenting the contents.

The senior accountant brought his laptop into the meeting room. We dragged a table over to be close to the area of the boxes and the senior accountant launched Excel on his laptop. The senior accountant stated that he would create an Excel table to be used for inventory purposes to track the contents, and if I were to go through each box in order and describe what each box contained, he would capture the information within the spreadsheet.

We started with the four numbered garbage bags that contained the contents of the trash bins out at the division. I opened the first bag and emptied the contents onto a table. Then I put on a pair of latex gloves to ensure I didn't get anything on my hands. The senior accountant captured the bag number and location where the bagged contents originated, and watched as I sifted through the trash contents. The bag came from the bin adjacent to the woman's desk, and contained no financial information. Plenty of dirty tissues, food wrappers, used coffee cups with empty sugar packets, and other delightful things, but nothing financial that would help us identify if and how funds were being diverted. With all the contents placed back into the garbage bag, I resealed the bag and placed it back on the floor. The senior accountant documented "nothing financial" within the spreadsheet. One bag down, three more to go.

LEARNING POINT

What's in your audit bag? Think about the procedures you may need to perform in a financial investigation, such as sifting through the contents of garbage pails or a dumpster (hopefully not that often). How prepared would you be if you needed to perform these types of procedures? For instance, do you have disposable rubber gloves in your bag? Would you want to sift through others' garbage contents with your bare hands? And what if you find something in that garbage collection? How will you collect it, and how will you secure it? A pair of forceps would be handy to keep you from having to touch it, and help keep your fingerprints off the evidence, as would large, clear plastic bags to allow the evidence to be collected and preserved, and even be photocopied through the bag if needed. Think about the types of evidence you may be required to collect, secure, and preserve, both documents and electronic information, and be prepared out in the field.

Bag number two came from the office manager's desk area. We already knew there was financial information pertaining to the opening of a new bank account in his trash, as it was identified during the collection process yesterday. I emptied the contents onto the table and sifted through the trash. There was much more financial information in this trash bin, including a blank deposit slip and an envelope from the new bank. Deposit receipts dated within the last few days were also found, along with paperwork and offers commonly found in envelopes containing vendor invoices. The only interesting items found in the bag related to the new bank account, especially when the office manager had stated yesterday that there were no new or other known bank accounts. I placed the bank-related items into a clear protective sleeve, and labeled the sleeve with an evidence label, identifying the bag number and location where the items originated. I put the remaining trash items back into the bag, sealed the bag, and returned it back to its spot on the floor. Two bags down and nothing earth shattering found yet.

Bag three, collected in the conference room area, was much like the first bag. A whole lot of food-type trash but nothing financially related. Bag four, however, contained the contents of the controller's garbage bin. As I emptied the contents onto the table, I saw portions of a credit card statement in the pile. I also saw vendor invoices and other financial information. I carefully sorted the contents between financial and non-financial, and returned the non-financial items back into the bag. Then I sorted through the financial items, and the senior accountant came around the table to watch over my shoulder. Credit card offers torn in half, many empty used envelopes, and a piece of a credit card statement with the last four digits of the account number identified (the beginning portion contained all asterisks).

I placed the credit card statement into a clear protective sleeve, marked the sleeve with an evidence label, and returned the remaining items into the bag. I sealed the bag and returned it to the floor, a bit disappointed that I didn't find more in the contents of the four trash bins. I set the credit card statement aside to later match the account number, or at least the last four digits of the account number, to the credit card statement Tim had provided me with at the onset of the investigation.

I left the senior accountant alone in the room with the boxes and bags, and walked over to Tim's office. I waited in his open doorway until he finished his phone call. Then I asked if I could ask him a question regarding his closed-door meeting with the controller yesterday at the division. I asked Tim to describe what happened with the controller from the time he was escorted to his office until he left the building. Tim said the controller wanted to retrieve his personal items and information from his office, and indicated he maintained personal items in his desk. Tim said he escorted the controller back to his office, closed the door and stayed with him the entire time. Tim stated the controller worked at his desk and sorted through piles of papers that he had retrieved from the desk drawers. Tim said he made a stack of papers on the top of his desk, and as he flipped through the papers, he put some into a separate pile. He also put some items back into the drawers, and threw others away in his trash bin. Tim said he watched as the controller removed papers from envelopes, ripped the envelopes in half, and threw them into the trash bin. When the controller was finished, he put the stack of papers from his desk into his briefcase, and walked over to the shelves on the wall. He flipped through the stacks of papers on the shelves, and went through the papers much faster than when he went through his desk. Tim said when he finished looking through the shelves, the controller walked out of the office with his briefcase full of papers, with Tim following right behind.

I asked Tim if he saw or recognized any of the papers the controller put into his briefcase. Tim said the controller said he kept personal bank account statements in his desk, and that the papers he was taking with him related to his personal accounts. I asked Tim if he flipped through the papers the controller was taking to verify what the controller was saying. Tim recognized someone should have reviewed the papers before allowing the controller to leave, in order to ensure they were in fact the personal bank statements for his accounts, and not critical evidence regarding the credit cards or undisclosed bank accounts. In retrospect, someone should have reviewed everything the controller was taking. We both realized that the papers the controller frantically reviewed and removed were likely related to this potential scheme that he perpetrated, and that he took the very evidence we were seeking out the door with him in his briefcase.

● ● ●

I returned to the meeting room. The senior accountant was still in the room, typing on his laptop. I now needed to focus my efforts on the 26 boxes that waited to be inventoried, knowing the information relating to the potential fraud was likely not in any of the boxes. It likely left with the controller as he walked away from the building, never to be seen again. It also made me wonder why the controller spent so much time going through the papers in his desk, and then leaving his laptop behind. I figured if there was any evidence remaining, it likely wasn't on his laptop, or he would have taken it with him.

I opened and reviewed the contents of each box, following them in sequential order, while the senior accountant captured information for each box. One by one, I went through each box, finding deposit details for several fiscal years, paid invoices, payroll records, and financial reports of various types. I knew from Tim that the division utilized the QuickBooks accounting system for their bookkeeping, and the reports I found had that familiar QuickBooks look and feel to them. I also knew from personal experience that QuickBooks was one of the easiest accounting packages in existence to manipulate at ease, to reflect whatever activity and results were desired. It remains one of the only systems to allow an unrestricted user to change or delete transactions at virtually any time, leaving little or nothing in the form of an audit trail. Even a basic-level user who spent just a little time with the system could figure out how to delete the audit logs, removing any possible discovery of changed or deleted transactions.

LEARNING POINT

QuickBooks, especially the later versions, includes some great tracking logs and audit trails. Most unsophisticated users do not even know these files exist, tracking user transactions, changes, deleted transactions, and voided transactions. The logs and trails, though, can be disabled or turned off by a sophisticated user. The files can also be purged, permanently deleting the contents of the logs and trails. The first thing to look for is the existence of the information. If present, then the user likely never knew about the tracking, or didn't have a chance to delete the contents. However, if the target was tipped off before access to QuickBooks had been gained, all may still not be lost. This is when you hope the organization has backups of the drive containing QuickBooks. You may have to go back a week or even further, but if a decent backup strategy is in place, you may find that you can gain access to the QuickBooks files at a date prior to when the files were purged or deleted. If no backups exist before the deletion occurred, you are likely out of luck. That's another reason why the element of surprise is important in these types of cases.

I located bank statements and reconciliations in one of the boxes. I sorted the folders by account number, and read the bank and account numbers of each statement to the senior accountant, who captured them for the inventory. I never located any further information relating to the new account at the new bank as identified by papers found in the office manager's trash bin.

Inventorying the boxes took the better part of the day, and by the last box I had a pretty good sense of what was collected and what information was still needed, only to be obtained through some other means. No credit card statements or accounts were located in the boxes. I did find the manual multi-part cash receipts books that were used to record payments as they were received. The three-part, pre-numbered receipt books contained the pink receipt copies, while the white and yellow copies of each receipt had been properly removed from the books. The most recent books were found in boxes containing information collected from the office manager's desk, and the older, completed receipt books were located in boxes also containing the receipts and deposit details of past periods.

LEARNING POINT

Many organizations have abandoned the use of manual, carbonless, multi-part, pre-numbered receipt books, only to be replaced by computer-generated receipts, or worse, providing no receipt and indicating to customers that their canceled check is their receipt. Quite often in organizations that continued to utilize the manual receipt books, those receipts were the only means to identify that a potential problem was occurring. The receipt books provide a means for comparing the funds collected on any given day to the funds posted to the system, and also to the funds that actually made it to the bank in the form of deposits.

To strengthen the internal controls created by using the manual receipt books, a supervisory-level person independent of collecting payments and completing the receipts should retrieve the receipt books at random intervals, and compare the collections up to that point in time with the completed receipts in the book. This measure will not only add a level of deterrence, as the employees never know when the book will be pulled and reconciled, but would also test for compliance with the receipting requirement.

In the case of a potential theft of cash receipts or payments received by an organization, the receipt books could prove invaluable. Receipts in the

(Continued)

(*Continued*)

books could be identified for targeted periods, and compared to payments posted within the accounting system as well as to the actual bank deposits.

In the case of lapping, where a payment from one customer is used to offset the outstanding balance of another customer to conceal the diversion of the payment made by the first customer, the receipt book would identify the customer who provided the payment. In comparing the manual receipt to the system entries, the payment either would match customers or it wouldn't. Now if the manual receipt books were eliminated to streamline the process or remove a "redundant" step, identifying a lapping scheme would be much more difficult, if not impossible.

FRAUD FACTS

Lapping is the fraudster's version of "robbing Peter to pay Paul" skimming. It is the extraction of money from one account to cover shortages in another account. For example, a fraudster steals the payment intended for customer A's account. When a payment is received from customer B, the thief credits it to A's account. And when customer C pays, that money is credited to B. Repeated many times, lapping is difficult for the dishonest employee to keep track of. As a result, almost all lapping schemes quickly reveal themselves. All material cash misappropriations send telltale signs: reduced cash combined with increased expenses and/or decreased revenue. Most lapping occurs because of inadequate control over incoming payments. The following are some classic "red flags" of lapping:

- Excessive billing errors
- Slowing accounts receivable turnover
- Excessive write-offs of accounts receivable
- Delays in posting customer payments
- Accounts receivable detail doesn't agree with general ledger
- A trend of decreasing payments on accounts receivable
- Customer complaints[1]

I pulled the receipt books from their respective boxes, and placed them into envelopes. I marked each envelope with an evidence label, and identified the box number and origination of each envelope's contents.

• • •

It was about 2:30 in the afternoon. I had been through all of the boxes, at least preliminarily, and the senior accountant had captured a decent inventory of what we had collected. Much of the information appeared to be unrelated to the allegations, and we started to think about how to separate the information that might be pertinent from that which could be returned to the division.

It was at about that time that I received a call from the human resource director. She had gone out to the division first thing in the morning and was working with the remaining employees to minimize the effects of yesterday's visit, as well as to help keep the division running as close to normal as possible. Tim, too, was busy throughout the day dealing with the banks to effect a change in authorized signers to allow the division to continue operations without having to open completely new bank accounts. While no further banking would be allowed through the controller, an additional authorized person would need to be added to all accounts. That person was Tim, and once authorized, Tim would be temporarily responsible for things like signing the division's checks, authorizing payroll, and effecting bank transfers as needed. The remaining staff could continue to receive, process, and deposit payments under Tim's guidance and review.

The human resource director indicated to me that she was having a real problem with the woman who was present yesterday when we arrived, in that she could not get anything accomplished without crying. She said she spent most of the day crying, and nothing she would tell her could get her to come around. She asked me if I had any suggestions regarding what she could do with the woman.

Due to the lateness of the afternoon, I didn't see any point getting into the car and driving over to the division to talk with the woman. I figured if she had cried most of the day, then she needed more time before I could make any inroads in talking with her. I told the human resource director that she should send her home for the rest of the day, and that I would want to meet with her first thing in the morning. With that the human resource director walked her out and the woman left for the remainder of the day.

I called the human resource director back to talk about how things went at the division for the day, and to see how the other employees who were not present yesterday reacted to the news. The human resource director said not much had happened at the division today, much as if the division's office had been closed for a holiday.

She said two other employees, both women, had come in and wanted to talk privately with her to learn firsthand what had happened yesterday, and most importantly, what had led to yesterday's abrupt visit. She also said both individuals asked to meet with me privately the next time I came out to the division.

I asked the human resource director to set up meetings for tomorrow, as I would be out there anyway meeting with the first woman, and said that I would have time to meet each person during that visit. I also indicated that I would be bringing back some of the information to the division that was deemed not pertinent to the investigation the next day for filing back where it originated.

I went back to work with the boxes and bags, focusing on segregating the pertinent information from all the rest of the boxes and bags. As I revisited each box in numerical order, I identified the items within each box deemed pertinent. I removed the contents deemed not pertinent, and placed them in a new box. The box was labeled, and the pertinent contents remained in the original numbered box. In the case where an entire box was deemed non-pertinent, the box was set aside with the new boxes for return to the division.

LEARNING POINT

Space is often a commodity, especially secured space, such as within an evidence room. Often a significant amount of information is collected in the field, and unless the information is sorted to segregate the pertinent evidence from everything else, a few investigations will consume all your space. In many cases, much of the collected information will not be needed to support the goals of the investigation. Why consume the precious space with this unneeded information? Segregate the information, document how it was segregated, and prepare to return or otherwise provide alternative storage means for the collected information that won't be required to support the engagement. This will reduce the amount of space required to maintain the pertinent evidence in the secured environment.

The senior accountant documented the segregation of the contents, as well as the new boxes filled with non-pertinent information. The spreadsheet originally consisted of 26 boxes and 4 bags, and now built off of those items were the new boxes established for non-pertinent contents to enable a complete tracking of the contents of each box and bag. Once completed, we stacked all the boxes and bags to be returned to the division tomorrow, and matched the stacked boxes and bags to the spreadsheet inventory. We then moved the original boxes, one by one, back into the storage room, once again matching the remaining boxes to the spreadsheet inventory.

The storage room was shut and secured for the night, and I placed a piece of evidence tape across the doorjamb to ensure no one went into the room until I returned late tomorrow, or the following day.

As we were preparing to end our day, my cell phone rang. I found my phone and recognized the number. It was the computer forensic specialist calling.

CHAPTER 5

ELECTRONIC EVIDENCE CONSIDERATIONS (COMPUTERS, FILES, AND COMMUNICATIONS)

The computer forensic specialist was calling from his cell phone. He indicated they had imaged all four computers, replaced the original hard drives with images, and tested each computer, and was on his way to our location to return the computers for use by the division. I had forgotten until then that the division had run all day without the use of any computers. I looked at the clock and it was late afternoon. The building would not be open for too much longer unless Tim stayed to allow us to work late. I told him to call me when he reached the building. I didn't realize the drives would be imaged and returned so quickly, and now I was anxious to learn if they had spent any time analyzing each computer's contents. If so, I wanted to know what they found, if anything, before I left for the night.

Within a half hour, I received another call on my cell from the computer forensic specialist, who indicated he was out in the parking lot with the computers. The senior accountant and I went out to meet him. We each carried a computer from the truck back into the building. We brought the computers into the same room we used for inventorying all the boxes and bags and went out to get the other two computers. Once all four computers were in the room, we spoke with the computer forensic specialist about the process they followed and the procedures they had performed. He had brought in the notepad that he had with him yesterday.

I asked him what procedures had been performed regarding the computers and electronic evidence since he collected them from the division yesterday. He said when he left he went straight to their building and brought each computer into their computer lab. After, he labeled each computer, and worked with their technician to open and identify the type of drive within each computer. He documented the details in his notebook while the technician reviewed the components of each computer. He said the technician then made two forensic images of each drive, and verified the contents of each image. Once verified, the original hard drives were removed from the computers, labeled, placed into cases, and stored within their electronic evidence cabinets contained within their forensic lab. He said one set of the imaged drives was set aside to be examined, and one set of imaged drives was installed into the computers. The technician then booted and tested each computer to ensure the imaged drive operated properly. Each computer was then put aside within the evidence room to be returned the next day. He said the details of each drive along with the tracking numbers assigned to the original and imaged drives were documented within his notebook.

The computer forensic specialist said the technician then installed one of the imaged drives into his lab computers and began to review the drive contents. He indicated the technician looked for deleted files and e-mails, as well as Internet histories, and printed the inventories of each hard drive. He said the technician did the same procedures for all four drives, making careful notes specific to each drive. Then, the imaged drives were filed with the original drives within their electronic evidence cabinets.

LEARNING POINT

What happens to the original hard drives in the seized computers is very important. Often the collection and imaging is completed prior to involvement by law enforcement, as insufficient information may have been collected and analyzed up to that point to identify if a crime has been committed. In many cases, law enforcement will never be involved in the engagement, by design and desire of the victim organization. However, should law enforcement become involved at some point after evidence has been collected, they will be very interested in how the chain of custody

(Continued)

over the evidence has been preserved. This is especially true when electronic information is involved. Having computer drives imaged and returned to the original computer for continued use may not be sufficient. Law enforcement, prosecutors, and courts often will want to know where the actual original drive is, and not an image. Measures should be contemplated and discussed to determine if the original drives will be critical in the case, or if forensic images will suffice. When in doubt, I recommend erring on the side of preserving the actual original drives, tapes, and other electronic media, and returning an image or copy back for subsequent use.

As he finished, he connected a monitor, keyboard, and mouse to the oldest computer seized and booted it up. As it booted up, he reviewed his notes and explained that the computer didn't have much relevant information on it. There were no files identified that were newer than two years ago, and as far as they could tell the computer was never connected to e-mail or the Internet. He ran down the file directory structure and said that the computer likely hadn't been used in quite some time. Once the computer had booted and was ready, he showed the senior accountant and me the contents of the hard drive. He showed us where data files had been maintained and the age of the files. I took some notes regarding the computer, the date and time it was returned to us, and other things the computer forensic specialist was saying about this computer.

We shut down the computer, disconnected the monitor, keyboard and mouse, and placed the computer with the boxes and bags to be returned to the division the next day.

Next, we connected and booted the second computer. Much like the first one, this computer looked pretty old. As he read from his notes, he indicated the files on this computer hadn't been accessed in at least a few years. However, this computer had been previously connected to send and receive e-mails, as well as to the Internet. He said that once the drives were imaged, they searched through the hard drive looking for any potentially relevant information or files. They were unable to locate any such pertinent information on the computer. As with the first one, he showed us the hard drive contents and highlighted the aged dates on the files themselves. I wrote the date and time in my notebook and shut down the computer. I disconnected the monitor, keyboard and mouse, and placed it on the floor with the other computer to be returned to the division.

The third computer was the desktop used by the woman who was present when we arrived yesterday to collect evidence. As I connected the monitor, keyboard, and mouse, I noted the network card installed and remembered that there were no network cards installed in the first two, older computers. I asked the computer forensic specialist what he found regarding a network at the division. He said the division was set up as a peer-to-peer local area network, configured so that one computer (the office manager's) would serve as the host or file server for any other connected computers. He indicated the only other computer that he observed connected via network cards and cables was the computer used by the woman. He also said he found no wireless devices, including wireless Internet, and that the Internet service was connected to the office manager's computer. The woman gained access to the Internet through access to the office manager's computer over the peer-to-peer network.

Once the computer was ready, he showed us the contents of her hard drive. She maintained a database of members of the division, but otherwise had little beyond the typical Microsoft Office suite of programs. The data files on her hard drive were minimal and mainly administrative in nature and her Internet activity contained the expected level of personal site visits. We reviewed her e-mail traffic and contacts and found nothing unusual. All in all, nothing exciting or helpful was found on her hard drive.

● ● ●

With one computer remaining, I was hoping that the computer forensic specialist was saving the best for last. Otherwise, I realized that the potential existed that I had caused the organization to spend its funds seizing, preserving, and analyzing computers only to result in nothing useful to help resolve the allegations. It's a double-edged sword—damned if you do and damned if you don't. My philosophy is to err on the side of caution and preserve computer drives rather than run the risk that relevant evidence gets lost forever because of deletion, destruction, or misplacement.

Still, it would be great if they had found things of interest on the office manager's computer. The forensic computer specialist connected the computer and booted it up, then flipped through his notebook as it warmed up. He said they found a significant amount of personal e-mails and Internet activity, showing that the office manager spent a large portion of his time doing things personal in nature using the division's computer. He said much of the Internet and e-mail traffic related to clubs and organizations which the office manager must have belonged to or at least had a strong interest in. He showed us where the office manager had used the Internet to access the bank accounts of the division. Then, he showed us inquiries made to credit card companies and where someone using this computer had logged into credit card sites on a regular basis.

We saw that the division's QuickBooks accounting system was installed on the office manager's computer and the data files resided on his hard drive. The date stamp on the QuickBooks data file was yesterday's date, which meant someone at the division had been in QuickBooks yesterday prior to our arrival. We attempted to access the QuickBooks company files, but when the program started, we were prompted to enter the password. I retrieved my notebook and found the password the office manager had supplied me with yesterday. When I entered the password, it didn't work. I tried in it caps, lowercase, and combinations of both in case it was case sensitive. Nothing worked. We tried guessing at some obvious passwords, but none of them worked either. Big surprise—the office manager had provided me with a false password. We tried various other common passwords, but to no avail.

FRAUD FACTS

Sources for typical passwords can be found through common password lists as well as notes taped anywhere around the computer user's area, including under the keyboard and on the side of the monitor. The more stringent the password requirements, the more likely the passwords will be documented somewhere within the work area.

10 Most Commonly Used Passwords Online

PC magazine's May 8, 2007 issue listed the 10 most commonly used passwords online:

(Continued)

(*Continued*)

10. Password
9. 123456
8. qwerty
7. abc123
6. letmein
5. monkey
4. myspace1
3. password1
2. blink182
1. (your first name)[1]

I left the forensic computer specialist with the senior accountant and walked out to my car to retrieve a USB drive contained within my field bag I kept in the car. The USB drive contained various utilities and programs I have accumulated throughout my experience, mainly shareware, freeware, and other downloads obtained from the Internet. Included in my collection was a utility I found to remove the passwords from QuickBooks files.

LEARNING POINT

The Internet is a great resource for information and tools. A simple search using key terms can reveal resources often free of charge that come in extremely handy. Password-breaking programs and utilities are one such tool. Before calling technical support or buying software available to undo a user's password, I search the Internet for a solution. I frequently find articles, posts, and helpful information directly related to the package involved, provided by individuals who have encountered the same issue. Shareware solutions, utilities and programs written and distributed through the Internet, are frequently available for downloading, often free of charge. My experience with these programs is that they work as described. The fact is—they work too well. If someone with malicious intentions wants to break through user passwords, the same programs would allow them similar access.

I returned to the room and inserted my USB drive into the computer. I copied the file onto the hard drive, and launched the file. I selected the QuickBooks data file and within seconds the utility identified the password. I removed the USB drive, re-launched Quick-Books, entered the password when prompted, and we were in. Even the forensic computer specialist was impressed with the utility.

The first thing I did was access the company setup area. Then, I reset the user password to no password. A new user would have to be properly established going forward once the computer was returned to the division, so for now it would be easier and more efficient to move in and out of QuickBooks without having to enter the password every time.

LEARNING POINT

Most people don't think about making their life easier with things like passwords. They write down the user ID and password, to ensure they will be provided access time and again as needed. A much simpler and more efficient approach to ensure access to the electronic information every time is to remove the password requirements from the user or system once initial access has been gained. Then the password will never be needed again, eliminating the risk of losing the password and also losing access to the system and information.

I generated trial balance reports (a listing of every account within QuickBooks along with the balance in each account) and general ledger reports (a complete history of every transaction within every account for the defined period of time). I scanned each report on the screen, formatted the reports to fit the paper size, and connected a printer to the computer. Next, I generated the reports so that I could review them, make notations, and identify any questionable accounts, transactions, or balances worthy of analysis.

I found that there was no obvious credit card activity within the financial reports. I accessed the chart of accounts (the listing of every individual account within the system) and did not identify any accounts used to record and track credit card activity. I accessed the vendor list as well as the "Other Names" list (mainly a vendor list for nonrecurring payments) within QuickBooks, and scanned each list for any credit card companies. I found that "United Alliance" was included within the "Other Names" listing. I highlighted "United Alliance" and generated a historical transaction report listing every transaction with this vendor. In seconds, the report details were on the screen. While I was thrilled that we had found any credit card activity within QuickBooks, I was also surprised by the low level of volume (four payments) that had been made to United Alliance throughout the past few years. The report covering a span of ten years showed only a few transactions with United Alliance, certainly not the level of transactions or dollar amounts that I expected based on the informant's information.

Each of the four transactions identified the check number associated with each payment. I went over to the senior accountant's laptop and searched his evidence inventory, looking for the box number that contained the bank statements. I went to the storage room, cut the seal on the door, and found the box within the stack. I searched through the box and found the folder containing the statements for the identified bank account. I scanned the monthly statements until I found the month for the first payment. Once located, I flipped to the canceled check images and found the image of the check payable to United Alliance. The canceled check corroborated the entry within QuickBooks, and contained the last four digits of the United Alliance account number on the memo field of the check.

I found the check images for the other three payments in the folder and brought the statements to the copier to make copies.

Once copied, I placed the originals into clear plastic sleeves, labeled each sleeve, and placed the originals back into the boxes for the time being.

I went back to the senior accountant's inventory and searched for the box number that contained the division's paid invoices. Having found the box number, I returned to the storage room. The box contained folders filed in alphabetical order by vendor name. I scanned through the box looking for any folders marked United Alliance. I went through the entire box to ensure the folder had not been misfiled out of sequence. There was no folder for United Alliance. I found a folder marked "C Misc" and thought the United Alliance statements could have been filed in this folder rather than in a separate folder as expected. I flipped through the contents and found no United Alliance statements. I surmised the statements must have been stored somewhere outside of the normal paid invoice filing system, somewhere we had failed to look, or more likely, that the statements had left in the stack of papers taken by the controller.

● ● ●

When I did the original inventory earlier in the day, I scanned the box contents long enough to recognize the box contained the paid invoices and bills. Since I was already going through the box, I flipped in more detail through all the folders of paid invoices in the box. As I pulled out each folder and reviewed the contents, I noticed that the folders at times had been reused, which is a common bookkeeping practice to minimize the number of folders purchased and used. All you had to do to reuse a file folder was turn the folder inside out and you had a new folder that you could use for a new vendor. The old tab label would be facing backwards in the file drawer, and the new folder name would be facing forward.

As I made it to the letter *G* folders, I found a reused folder that had an old folder description of "Credit Card." The existence of the old, reused folder showed that there had in fact been credit card activity at one time, and that likely the credit card statements and supporting information were maintained right in the paid invoice files, just as expected. This raised two questions. Where were the credit card statements that used to be maintained within this folder, and why were they removed to a new location outside of the paid bills folders?

The four payments identified within QuickBooks leading to the bank account and ultimately the reused file folder confirmed that credit card activity did in fact occur and that the circumstances surrounding the credit card activity were suspicious as reported by the informant. Good information, but not the home run we were hoping to find this early in the investigation.

I closed and locked the storage room and resealed the door frame with evidence tape. I rejoined the senior accountant and forensic computer specialist, who were still sitting in front of the office manager's computer reviewing files and e-mails. I shared with them the United Alliance credit card information from the boxes and we agreed that the information likely was included in the papers taken by the controller.

The forensic computer specialist collected his notebook, cables, and other tools and prepared to leave. He listed the four computers returned to us and had me sign the form acknowledging that we had received the four computers. As he walked back to his car, I indicated that I would be contacting him with the next steps, and that he should hold off performing any further procedures with the drives until he received further instructions. I also told him that the drives being held as evidence should remain in his possession until further notice.

I returned to the room with a blank USB drive from my car and copied the QuickBooks files from the office manager's computer. I knew once I copied the files, I could access the system and generate any reports needed using QuickBooks installed on my laptop. The computer was brought over to the area of the other computers and boxes to be returned to the division.

With all the evidence returned and secured in the storage room, I left the boxes and computers in the room with the senior accountant to update the inventory. Each computer and box prepared for return to the division was updated in the inventory and appropriately noted in the file to ensure proper tracking of each item.

● ● ●

I saw Tim in the hallway and followed him back into his office. I closed the door to his office and sat in the chair in front of his desk. I opened my notebook, and asked him how he had made out with the bank accounts. Tim said he was successful in freezing all the known accounts from any further activity, and that he had completed all the required forms the banks provided to add himself as an authorized signer on each account. Tim indicated that the changes would not take effect until each request was approved and updated into the bank's system, and that it would likely be another day or two until all the bank accounts had been updated, allowing him access to bank information. Tim said that in the meantime he had already started drafting requests for the various banks to be used to request information, such as copies of any missing bank statements and any other supporting information.

Tim said he saw that the forensic computer specialist had returned the computers, and he asked me how we had made out with the computers. I told him two of the computers, the older-looking desktops, were determined to be computers that had not been used in some time with nothing pertinent found on their hard drives. I also told him the computer used by the woman who was present during our visit contained nothing financial or pertinent to bank accounts or credit cards.

Tim then asked me about the office manager's computer. I told him that his computer was where the QuickBooks system resided and that it had been accessed as recently as yesterday. I told him they found that the office manager spent a significant amount of time and energy on personal activity conducted via e-mails and the Internet, most of which was related to groups, clubs, or organizations he likely belonged to. I shared with Tim how we accessed QuickBooks and were able to generate reports that revealed little or nothing at first, but then found four payments posted within QuickBooks to United Alliance. I told Tim how I traced the payments to the canceled check images and how I found the reused folder.

I asked Tim if he had heard that I needed to go out to the division to meet with the woman and with two other employees tomorrow, and how the woman had had significant emotional issues today that precluded her from performing anything useful. Tim said he had heard the same from the human resource director, and that she would be out at the division again tomorrow to coordinate the interviews.

We agreed that we had made significant progress in the two days we had spent thus far in this investigation.

I ended the day by loading all the boxes and computers into my car to be returned to the division in the morning. All of the information to be returned was no longer going to be treated as evidence and I was no longer concerned about maintaining the chain of custody for these items, at least from an evidentiary perspective. I knew I would have to park my car in the garage tonight and be sure to lock my car as well, to ensure that nothing happened to the boxes and computers until their safe return to the division tomorrow morning.

LEARNING POINT

Had the boxes and evidence been deemed pertinent or contained evidence, leaving them in a locked car may not be sufficient to ensure proper chain of custody, even if the car was locked in a closed garage. A risk of loss always exists in that the garage could catch fire, the car could be stolen, or the records could be stolen from the garage. Even if the stored items are not evidence, the client will suffer a loss and likely look toward you as a means of recovery for that loss. The question is this—why take on additional risk for mere convenience? Leave all client information and property in a secured and insured location, and only remove it to directly return it to the client. Also, whenever retrieving and returning information and property to a client, always have the information and property documented in some level of detail, and have someone at the client sign the form acknowledging the retrieval and return. Keep the signed forms in your files as evidence of what you retrieved as well as what you returned.

CHAPTER 6

INTERVIEWING
(RESPONDING TO TEARS)

Day three. I was driving out to meet the human resource director at the division. On my ride out, I called Tim to see if there were any updates since we departed last night and to check if there was anything specific he wanted me to talk about with the individuals during the interviews.

Tim indicated that he had spoken with the informant last evening and learned that the hysterical woman I was about to interview was close to the controller. Tim also said that the controller had been calling all the employees of the division to find out what he could about what was happening with our investigation. Tim told me the informant indicated they had received such a call from the controller, and that the controller told them he was being framed and believed the truth of the whole matter would come out eventually. The controller vowed to be back in his position before long, and would show everyone that he beat any allegations raised against him. Tim said the informant told him the woman was a very emotional person, and that she had her own issues outside of her employment within her personal and family life.

Tim asked me to see if any of the employees could shed some light on any financial issues or accounts handled exclusively by the controller or the office manager. I told Tim that was something I had already contemplated discussing with each person, and that I also wanted to know if there was anything else happening at the division. With that Tim wished me luck with the interviews, indicated he was available if he was needed, and asked that I call him later to provide him with an update.

I pulled into the parking lot and recognized the human resource director's car. I did not see any other cars and walked up the sidewalk to the front door. The human resource director was waiting at the door when I arrived. As I walked through the door, I asked her if any employees had arrived for work. She said that she was alone in the building, and that she had expected that the woman I was to interview initially would have been at work by now. I figured this was going to be another case of someone who scheduled a date and time to meet, only to then decide for whatever reason not to follow through with the meeting. It happens frequently in these types of matters.

I asked the human resource director how the day went yesterday at the division. She said it was a long day, especially meeting with the other employees at the division. She said the employees were anxious to meet with me today to discuss the whole matter. Two of the employees expressed concern for the future of their positions and the division, and would be looking for reassurances from me that their positions and employment would be continued going forward.

I asked the human resource director for the name of each person who worked at the division, as well as a brief history of each employee's employment. She provided me their names, dates of hire, and a brief description of each person's job responsibilities as best she knew from what she had gathered talking with the employees yesterday. I documented the employee names and the other information in my notebook so I would have it when I met with each person.

I asked her what office or room she recommended I use to meet with each individual to ensure their privacy and also to encourage them to speak candidly. She brought me to an empty office toward the back of the building. The office had a desk, two chairs in front of the desk, a big window behind the desk, and pictures on the wall. It appeared comfortable and nonthreatening, and was a good environment to get the employees to feel at ease to talk about the matter.

LEARNING POINT

Picking the interview environment is critical to the success of the interview. Determining where to interview someone will be based on the goals and objectives of the interview. For example, privacy may be important in some interviews, and less important in others. If you are trying to determine what

(Continued)

has been happening in the shipping area of a business, asking employees who work in that area may provide the best source of information. If you talk with them out in the shipping area, they may be more apt to answer your questions on an informal basis, as opposed to sitting across from you in a conference room, a place they have seen only once in their employment when they first were hired by the company. Conversely, if you were meeting with a target to seek an admission, you would want the individual out of the environment they control, where privacy and a lack of interruption is achieved. While not every interview will allow time and consideration for where best to meet, when possible, plan to meet in a location based on the goals of the interview.

While I waited for the woman to arrive, I carried in the boxes from my car. I brought them into the office area and asked the human resource director where she wanted me to leave them. I asked her not to put everything back where we had found it and to keep the boxes "as is" until we were further along in our procedures. She had me stack the boxes in a back office beyond the office manager's desk. It took several trips, but all the boxes were finally out of my car. I then started carrying in the computers. I started with the oldest ones and returned them back to where we had originally found them on Tuesday. Neither were connected or plugged in on Tuesday, so I saw no need to do anything different with them today.

I carried in the woman's computer and put it back on her desk. I connected the monitor, keyboard, mouse, network, and all the other cables and wires, and turned the computer on. As it booted up, I walked out to retrieve the last computer. I thought about how much easier it would have been if I had thought about bringing some type of cart. I put the last computer back on the office manager's desk, and connected all the wires and devices to it. I booted up the computer and watched as it ran through the boot process. Once it was finished, I entered the user ID and password the office manager had provided, and we gained access to the system. I walked over to the woman's desk and attempted to log into her computer. I did not have her password, so I decided to leave it where it was for the woman to log in when she arrived.

• • •

About a half hour after I arrived, I noticed the woman walking up the front walk toward the building. We watched her from the window as she approached the front door. She walked as if she had the weight of the world on her shoulders, her face long and hung low. The human resource director said it was pretty much how she looked all day yesterday, that is, when she wasn't crying, of course.

I opened the door and let her in, and her face was not red as if she had been crying. I introduced myself to her and asked her if she wanted anything before we talked for a while. She responded that she didn't need anything, so I led her down to the office where we were to meet. I had already arranged the two chairs in front of the desk to face each other and had put my notebook on the chair farthest from the office door.

LEARNING POINT

Another aspect of a successful interview is determining how the room will be arranged. Where you will sit, how you will position yourself, where the interviewee will sit, and how he will be positioned are aspects to be considered. Will the chairs be facing one another unobstructed, or will one chair be in front of a desk or table with the other on the other side? Does the interviewee's chair face the door, or does he have his back toward the door? How many chairs should there be in the room? Are there any distractions in the room that could affect the individual's attention span or stress level? What about windows? Should there be windows in the room, or should the walls be solid walls? And what should be on those walls? These individual details may contribute to the success of the interview. As with the location of the interview, the details in setting up the room should be considered in light of the goals of each interview.

She removed her outer coat, placed it on the hook on the back of the door and sat in the open chair facing me. Her head still hung low and heavy, but fortunately for me there were still no tears. I looked down to make sure my briefcase was down on the floor next to me. In my briefcase, I carry packets of tissues for times just like these when someone is likely to cry. Based on my experience and the number of times I have had individuals cry, I tend to keep tissue packets in my bag all the time. They have come in really handy over the years.

I started my rapport building by asking her for her name. When she provided it, I asked her how long she worked at the division. I continued along with this questioning to learn as much as possible about her, her position, and her responsibilities before I started to ask her anything about the office manager or the controller. We spent a good 15 minutes just talking about her history and responsibilities at the division and she maintained her composure the entire time.

I then asked her why she was so upset yesterday. That was the first sign I noticed that she went from calm and conversational to crying. I noticed her bottom lip start to quiver and her eyes well up. Her face went from flushed to pink and I reached down to grab the tissue packet that I knew was right down at my feet. As I handed her the tissues, she proceeded to let the tears flow.

After a minute or so, I asked her why she was getting so upset talking about the division. Between wiping tears, she said that she was very upset by the dramatic change and removal of the controller and office manager on Tuesday. She said she had worked with both of them very closely, and could not believe they were treated in this fashion. She also said she feared for her own job, and that something similar could happen to her at any moment like it had with them. With that short set of comments, more tears flowed.

I asked her if she thought Tuesday's procedures, the temporary removal of the controller and the office manager, the removal of the files, and the removal of the computers, were completely random. She just nodded and wiped away tears. I asked her if she thought the fact that she and the other employees were still at the division and were not placed on administrative leave was random. Again, she gave me a nod, but no verbal response. I told her that I was meeting with her to provide factual information about Tuesday's procedures to the extent that I could, to ensure that she and the other employees had all the facts, and that she could ask me any questions she had.

Then I asked her if she had any questions. She wiped her tears, and asked me why we did what we did on Tuesday. I told her that we needed to perform a financial review of the division, and that in order to preserve the integrity of the procedures, the integrity of the information itself, and the integrity of the individuals involved in running the financial aspects of the division, we decided to take over the division temporarily until we could complete our financial analysis. I told her that we had spoken with the controller and the office manager on Tuesday, and both were told that the best way to preserve their integrity and reputations, and allow an independent and objective analysis of the finances of the division to be completed, was to place them on paid leave, allowing them to separate themselves from the analysis yet continue to get paid as usual. I explained that it wasn't anything personal with either individual, but that it is customary to place individuals on paid leave until the outcome of the procedures. I referenced examples of government employees and civil servants (police officers, firefighters . . .), and how whenever any of these individuals gets involved in some sort of issue, they are almost always placed on some type of administrative duty or paid leave pending the outcome of the inquiry. She seemed to accept my analogy, or at least the tears seemed to stop and her color was back to normal, whatever normal might be for her. I cautioned her not to listen to things she heard or would hear about the matter, as it could be intentionally misleading, and to listen to the facts as I was presenting them. I told her that if she had questions going forward, she should contact the human resource director or me to ensure she received only accurate information.

FRAUD FACTS

Paid administrative leave is a temporary leave from a job assignment, with pay and benefits intact. Generally, the term is reserved for employees of non-business institutions such as schools, police, and hospitals. Usually, an employee is placed on administrative leave when a constituent (student, parent, patient, suspect, victim, etc.) makes an allegation of misconduct against them. Many institutions choose to remove the employee from the situation while investigating such allegations. Police officers are routinely placed on administrative leave after a shooting incident while an investigation is conducted. This does not imply fault on the part of the officer, and the vast majority of officers placed on leave for these reasons soon return to active duty.

I asked her if she had any involvement with the financial aspects of the division. She said the only thing she performed when the office manager was out or unavailable was to collect payments and complete receipts for any payments received. I asked her to walk me through the process she followed for collecting and documenting payments, and she provided me with her explanation. I asked her if she always provided a receipt for every payment received, and she stated she always provided a receipt from the manual, three-part receipt book. I asked her if anyone else collected or received payments besides her, and with that her face fell toward the floor. She said the office manager mainly collected the payments and processed them for deposits. I asked her what she did with the payments she received after she completed the receipts, and she said she provided all payments to the office manager for processing and depositing. She adamantly said she never made any of the deposits. I asked her if the office manager always completed receipts for payments he received, and while looking downwards, she said he did as far as she knew. I asked her if anyone else handled cash receipts, payments, and completed the receipts. She said the only two people she knew who handled any payments were the office manager and herself, and she did only when he was out or not available.

I asked her if she had any other involvement with any financial aspects of the division. She said she maintained the database to track the membership, and that she entered any payments that were receipted into the database. I walked her through my understanding of what she said, and she indicated that I had understood her process accurately. I asked her if she knew of any receipts or payments that came into the division that did not get a receipt, and therefore did not get entered into the database because there was no receipt for those receipts or payments. She said there were none as far as she knew, and went on to say that as far as she knew all receipts and payments were to be receipted. She reiterated that she posted all of the receipts and payments into the database using the receipt books as her source for data entry. I asked her if she ever tried to reconcile the receipts per her database for a specified period to postings within QuickBooks and the actual bank deposits for the same period. She said she had no responsibility to perform any such reconciliation, and had never been asked to perform one. She said she never had access to QuickBooks or the bank statements, nor did she need access to do her job. I asked her if the office manager or controller had ever asked for a report, or if either had direct access themselves, to generate a report to be reconciled. She said she had never provided any such report, and that as far as she knew neither had access to the database. She also said that whenever she took time off, the postings to the database would stack up, requiring days to catch up as no one else ever posted to the database. I told her going forward that had to be addressed, and that someone else besides her would need to be identified and trained on how to post to the database to provide a backup to her for the division.

I asked her if there were any other financial aspects she completed for the division. She said she also processed the credit card charges for payments received from members of the organization. I asked her to explain to me what that meant. She walked me though how the office manager primarily processed member payments paid via credit card, but in his absence, she processed the charges for members. I asked her if the credit card payments were documented within the receipt book, and she said when she did the charges she completed a receipt for the payment received. I asked her if everyone who handled the credit card payments processed them the same way she processed the payments, and she said they were all supposed to follow the same procedures.

I again asked her if there were any other financial aspects she completed for the division. This time I allowed a long pause before I looked at her, allowing her time to think if there was anything further she wanted to provide. She stated there was nothing further. I asked her if she was going to be able to move past what happened Tuesday and be able to perform her functions at the division while the matter was being resolved. She began to cry again and said she didn't know. I asked her why she was crying again. She said she couldn't stop thinking about Tuesday and every time she did she cried. I asked her if she had anything she wanted to tell me that she knew about, whether it was about herself or anyone else in the division, that I would eventually learn about anyway through the procedures being performed. She said she knew of nothing that she could tell me regarding anyone at the division. I said to her that if she didn't have anything to tell me, and that if she didn't know of anything regarding anyone else at the division that she should tell me, then there really should be no reason to worry about her job and her future at this time. I also told her that there should also be no real reason for her to break down and cry each time she thought about the matter. I told her that in a short period of time, the procedures being performed would be completed and things could return back to the way they were before Tuesday. I could tell she knew that was not going to be the case, but I could also tell that as long as she was going to hold back and protect whatever she likely knew behind her crying and emotional state, she would likely have to be removed to minimize further disruptions with the other remaining employees. I also knew that the whole crying thing could be an act to get onto paid administrative leave and remain at home, being paid, while the procedures were being performed.

I asked her one last time if there was anything that she wanted to add or discuss. She said she didn't have any further questions at this time. I thanked her for her time and for meeting with me, and asked her to try and focus on moving forward to continue performing her job at the division. She said she would try, and I told her that is all anyone could ask of her. With that I walked her back to her desk, and told her to call me if she should have any questions or issues she wanted to discuss. I noted the start and stop times of the interview in my notebook, as well as updated the rough notes I had taken during the meeting. I had spent close to an hour and a half with her during our meeting.

•　•　•

I located the human resource director working in a back office, sorting the division's mail of the last two days. I could tell she was anxious to hear what had happened in our discussion. She followed me back to the office where I had met with the woman. As I gathered my notebook and pen, I realized the first woman had taken my packet of tissues. Now what was I going to have available if any of the other employees that I needed to meet with today began to cry? I thought to myself, if she could steal my packet of tissues, what else could she have stolen (*a bit cynical and insensitive, I know*).

I provided the human resource director with a summary of the interview and told her that I couldn't tell if she was very emotional and truly traumatized by Monday's events or if she was playing the role to get the same deal as the controller and the office manager— stay at home and continue to get paid. I shared with her some of the woman's responses that were really nonresponses to my questions. I told her I was concerned about receipts and payments from members that may not have been documented with receipts provided for the payments received. I told her I was also concerned about the credit card payments received, and how they may not have been properly documented and recorded. She said the next employee was waiting to meet with me, and that the employee had a meeting out of the office this afternoon and therefore I should go and meet with her before she had to leave the building. I asked her to find a box of tissues that I could bring, at least in part, to the remaining meetings. She returned with a small box of tissues.

I found the next employee, another woman, working on her laptop at her desk. I introduced myself to her, and asked her if it would be a good time to meet. She indicated it would be a good time and I walked with her back to the same office I previously used. As with the last interview, I asked her for her name and other questions regarding her role and responsibilities at the division. I learned that her responsibilities focused on the program side of things and that she likely had no financial roles within the division. This confirmed the little I had learned of each individual at the planning meeting we held prior to Tuesday's mission.

I asked her how she was holding up since Tuesday's abrupt change in the office, and she said she was doing just fine. I watched her face and there was no sign that she was going to break down and cry. I asked her if the temporary changes that were made on Tuesday affected her in any way. She indicated they affected her only to the extent of who would be signing her paycheck and approving her expenses. I asked her who had done that in the past. She indicated the office manager previously reviewed and approved all expenses, as well as distributed the payroll checks to the employees. I assured her that someone would be filling that role in the interim and that the human resource director was on site at the division to ensure that things like those continued without any interruptions. I asked her if either the controller or the office manager had contacted her since Tuesday and she said she had received a call from the controller. She said he called because she was not in the office on Tuesday when the events transpired, and that he wanted to tell her personally about what had happened at the division. She provided me with a brief summary of what he told her and I told her it was close to what actually happened. As with the woman during the earlier interview, I provided her with a factual account of what had transpired, and indicated to her that if she had any questions or issues going forward, she should contact me or the human resource director to ensure she received the most accurate and factual information available.

I asked her if she noticed anything unusual or questionable with any employees at the division. I asked her if she had any further questions of me. She asked me if she was being looked at as being potentially involved in anything we were analyzing. I told her, as I told the previous woman, that nothing that occurred on Tuesday was random. I told her that if we thought that her files, computer, and position should be preserved, then her files and computer would have already been collected to be analyzed along with all the other records and computers, and that she would likely be out on paid administrative leave, similar to the controller and office manager.

I asked her if she would be able to continue functioning in her position while the matter was being resolved, and she said she saw no reason for her to do anything less. I thanked her for her time meeting with me and provided her my contact information. I asked her to call or e-mail the human resource director or me if she had any questions or if she had any issues she needed to discuss. She left the office and turned in the direction of her work area. I documented the start and end times of the meeting and added to the notes I had written in my notebook. We had spent about an hour together during the meeting.

• • •

Lunch time. I could not believe how fast the day was going by. I needed a break and I needed food. I found the human resource director working at the office manager's desk. I asked her if she needed to get lunch, and she held up a bagged lunch that she had brought with her. I told her I was going to head out for a sandwich, and that I would be back within a short period of time to continue meeting with the employees.

It was a much-needed break in the action, and the warm, sunny outdoors allowed me to clear my mind and absorb the information provided during the morning's interviews. I hoped the crying woman would snap out of it and be able to continue performing her job functions. That was direly needed to ensure the division continued to operate without further interruptions, but a big part of me knew that that wasn't likely to happen.

I walked back to the building, grabbed my notebook, and headed down the hall to meet with the other individual working in her office. I found her sitting at her desk typing on a laptop computer. I introduced myself, and asked her if she had time to meet with me. She said she was waiting to meet with me. I asked her to follow me to the office I had been previously using.

Once seated, I asked her for her name and to provide me with a brief description of what she did at the division. She provided her name, and indicated she was responsible for various programs. I asked her if she knew what was happening at the division. She said she knew only that we had come out on Tuesday, the controller and office manager were put out on leave, and that records and computers were taken away. I asked her if she had any financial responsibilities, and she said the extent of her financial duties was to collect program fees from members. I also asked her to describe what that meant and how it worked. She said that some of the programs she ran were included in the cost of membership to the organization, and that other programs had a separate charge for participation. With regard to the separate-charge programs, she would register the members for the programs and collect the fee from each participant. I asked her how the funds were tracked for each program, and she said a listing of the participants was maintained by her. Once the program ran, she would summarize the funds and forward them to the office manager for recording and depositing. I asked her if she ever did the recording and/or depositing, and she replied that she merely collected and tracked the member payments. She said the office manager handled the deposits once he received the program envelope containing the payments.

I asked her if she ever reconciled, or was ever asked to reconcile, the program tracking she performed with the recording and deposits performed by the office manager. She indicated she had never completed any such reconciliation, nor was she ever asked to generate any reports to be used to perform such a reconciliation.

I asked her if she had access to QuickBooks or performed any recording within QuickBooks. She stated she had no access and had nothing to do with QuickBooks. I asked her who tracked and reconciled the programs that included a separate charge when she was on vacation or otherwise unavailable. She said the program information, including payments, would sit and wait until she returned to perform the necessary bookkeeping. I asked her if there were any other financial aspects to her employment. She said there were none.

I asked her if she incurred any business expenses on behalf of the organization, and if she in fact did incur costs, how did she submit the costs for reimbursement? She said there were two ways that she could incur costs on behalf of the programs. The first was to use her personal funds to pay the costs. Then, she could complete an employee reimbursement form, attach the receipts, and submit it to accounting for payment. She said the second was for her to simply charge the cost to the business credit card, and forward the receipts from the purchase to the office manager. The office manager would then match the receipts with the credit card statement when it came in. She said she forwarded all her credit card slips to the office manager.

I asked her what the current status was on the corporate card. She said the controller had shut down the charge card account within the past two weeks, and that she had turned the card into him at that time. I asked her what type of card it was, and she said it was a United Alliance card. I asked her if she knew who else had a card, and she said that to the best of her knowledge, the only cardholders were herself, the office manager, and the controller.

I asked her what types of things she charged to the card, and as I watched her prepare to respond to my question, I noticed her bottom lip start to quiver. Her composure up to that point was good and there was no sign of potential crying. Then, I asked a very simple question about her use of the charge card.

The first single tear ran down the left side of her face. I reached down and grabbed the tissue box and extended the box to her. I waited for her to wipe the tear and remained silent to see how she would answer my question. She started by telling me how much she needed the job and that she could not afford to lose her health benefits. She said that she was having significant issues and that if she were to lose her job and her health-care insurance, she would have no way of dealing with her expenses and prescriptions. More tears ran down both sides of her face.

I asked her why her use of the corporate charge card with her receipts provided and approved by the office manager would lead to her losing her job and her benefits. She said that she had the controller's permission to charge, on an occasional basis, her prescriptions and other minor personal expenses. I asked her if she ever provided reimbursement to the division for the personal charges and she said that the controller never asked for any reimbursements. She said the office manager reviewed and approved her charges, and the controller signed the checks paying the credit card statements, so both of them knew that there were personal charges at times on the card. Yet, she said they never asked for any reimbursements from her.

I asked her if anyone else used the corporate card for personal purposes. She said that she never saw the monthly statements and would have had no way of knowing if any other charges were made by other cardholders to the account. I asked her why she charged personal items to the card paid through the division, and she said she had no other means of keeping up at times with her expenses and prescription costs. I asked her if she knew how much was charged that was personal in nature and also how long she had been using the card for personal use. She said she thought her occasional personal charges started some time in the past year or two. She also said she had no idea how much was charged personally, but that it couldn't be all that much, because she used it only occasionally when she had no other means of making a payment.

I thanked her for providing me with her information and asked her if she knew of any other financial issues occurring with anyone at the division. She said her only involvement with finances was with the program fees and the credit card usage, and that she tracked and remitted to the office manager all of the program fees she collected. She said once she gave the payments to him, he was responsible for recording and depositing them. I asked her if she had any questions of me at this time. She began to cry again and asked what would happen next based on what she had told me about the credit card. I told her that I would provide the information to the human resource director, and that I wasn't sure what the next steps would be in the matter. I asked her if she happened to have any of the credit card statements or any other information pertaining to the United Alliance credit card. She said she had none of those records, and that the monthly statement was received in the mail and opened by the office manager, consistent with all the other bills that were received at the division. I asked her if she knew where the office manager maintained the credit card statements, and she said he maintained a folder in his desk with all the statements in it. She said whenever there was a question regarding a charge on the card, she would go to the office manager who would retrieve a folder from the right drawer of his desk. I knew she was describing the folder I had found that was labeled credit card but had been recycled and reused for another vendor.

I thanked her for her time, and provided her with my contact information. I told her she should contact me or the human resource director if she had any further questions or wanted to provide any additional information. I walked her back to her desk, and returned to the office to gather my thoughts. I sat at the desk and updated my notes in my notebook, thinking how I was going to get access to the monthly credit card statements to determine the extent to which she had been charging personal purchases. I thought to myself that her admission was not what I was expecting from the interview. I expected her interview would be much like the one I had completed just before lunch. There was obviously more happening at the division than was known or provided by the informant. I wondered why the office manager and controller would allow her to charge personal items on the card, and also about the fact that the office manager had obviously lied to me once again about the existence of credit cards. That interview had lasted more than an hour, and I let her keep the box of tissues knowing she would be the last interview I was doing today.

• • •

I finished updating my notes and reconnected with the human resource director. We sat in the private office. I shared with her what the employee had just provided in the interview. Needless to say, she was as surprised as I was by the information. We both knew a decision would have to be made regarding her employment status, and whether to put her on paid administrative leave until the investigation was completed. The human resource director said there had been issues between the controller and the woman in the past, but that the details of those issues could not be shared with me. That told me there was some kind of history between the two of them, providing a possible explanation for the allowance to charge personal items. Now I began to wonder how much in personal charges she had made to the corporate card.

We decided we should provide an update to Tim and to legal counsel with these latest developments and called Tim from the office. When Tim answered the phone, I provided him with a summary of the day's meetings. I told him that a credit card account with United Alliance definitely existed within the division, and that one individual so far admitted to using the card for personal purposes without reimbursing the division. I told him I had no way of knowing how much was charged on the card, or if any of the other employees beyond the office manager and the controller had access to the card. After my summary, I indicated that I thought it would be a good idea to bring counsel up to date on our progress, as I had not spoken with counsel directly since the initial procedures two days earlier. Tim agreed and he connected counsel to our conference call. I provided a similar summary of the two-days' progress with counsel on the call, and suggested that a decision would have to be made regarding the employment status of the woman who admitted using the corporate card for personal use. I provided my recommendation, which was to place her on paid administrative leave, as we did with the controller and office manager, which would buy us time to retrieve the credit card statements and quantify the personal expenses charged to the division's credit card. The human resource director raised a concern regarding the continued operations of the division with yet one fewer employee who had been performing certain program-related functions for many years. She said the loss of the woman crying all the time coupled with the potential of putting this other employee on paid leave would leave the division with one original employee. She wanted to know from Tim who would be brought in to run the division while the staff remained on paid leave.

Tim said he was already working on that issue and was close to identifying a solution to put things in place during the investigation. Tim asked the human resource director if she could continue to go out to the division on a daily basis for a while longer, which would allow him time to complete a plan for running the division during the investigation. She agreed to continue until Tim had a plan to put in place. We agreed that in hindsight we should have done a better job addressing business continuity issues when we met during the planning of the investigation. I reminded them of a resource I identified earlier that could step in and help during the interim, but Tim wanted to spend a little more time working on a plan that would not require the use of any outside resources.

I asked the group if we had enough information to start drafting a request for the credit card statements. I indicated the credit card statement provided to Tim by the informant showed that the card was in the controller's name and not in the name of the division. I added that United Alliance would *only* provide the account information and monthly statements to the account owner and *only* to the address on file with the account. I said I thought any request made by anyone other than the controller would not be honored by United Alliance. We discussed other options to solicit the credit card information, such as through a subpoena. However, a subpoena would have to be issued in relation to a civil complaint or lawsuit, and since no such action had been initiated in this matter, the use of a subpoena was not available to us. That pretty much left us the only option of asking the controller to provide us with the United Alliance statements and account information, and since he likely took that paperwork with him from his desk on the first day at the division, the chances of him simply providing us with the statements seemed remote at best.

LEARNING POINT

Due to all the new privacy laws in response to the frequency of identity theft, obtaining financial information such as bank and credit card records to conduct a financial investigation has become difficult if not impossible without involving law enforcement who can apply for search warrants. The three means typically available are by a request of the account owner, by subpoena, and by search warrant. Once a target agrees to "cooperate," either directly or through her attorney, the next thing one should consider is how her cooperation will gain you access to needed information. Bank accounts, credit card accounts, tax returns, and any other protected information may be accessible by seizing the moment when cooperation is offered, and having the target sign request forms for this information. Allowing too much time to pass between her offer and your request could lead to her reconsideration, or her changing her mind, about cooperating with you.

We agreed to leave the United Alliance statement issue for now, and to continue looking for other information to piece together what, if anything, happened financially within the division. Per counsel's advice, the employee who admitted using the credit card for personal use was to remain an active employee pending the identification and quantification of her personal use of the credit card. The rationalization behind that decision included the fact that the office manager and controller had approved her usage, the card no longer existed as far as we knew, and the division needed to continue to operate until Tim identified a better operating plan (with or without her).

We ended our call with Tim and counsel, and remained in the office discussing the next steps to be taken to resolve this matter. I asked the human resource director what her thoughts were in bringing the office manager back for an interview. She thought it would be a good idea, if he would agree to come in, to see if he would provide anything. She was especially interested in his reaction and responses when we showed him that some of the information he provided initially was wrong or misleading. She also said she had her doubts that he would agree to come in for a meeting. I told her it was worth a shot, and asked her to get me his contact information.

She returned to the office with his personnel file and provided me with his home phone number. She indicated she thought he still lived at home with his parents. I remembered our brief interactions and thought he was a bit old to be still living with his parents. I asked her if he was married, and she said to her knowledge he was not. I asked if he had a girlfriend, and she stated she wasn't aware of a girlfriend. I called the number she provided for the office manager. I didn't get any response except from his answering machine. I left a message identifying myself as the accountant who had spoken to him during the initial visit earlier in the week, and saying that I wanted to meet with him, at his convenience, if he would be willing to meet. I asked him to call me at the division, and provided him with the phone number along with the date and time of my call. I asked him to call me back either way so I knew that he had received the message.

I asked the human resource director if she thought he would call back, and she said she thought he wouldn't call back. I told her I disagreed. I said I thought he was likely sitting home wondering what was happening in the case over the past couple of days, and that the unknown was likely stressing him out. I said I thought he would call back and would schedule a time to meet, but not to provide us with any information. I said I thought he would agree to meet us to learn what we knew and where we were heading with this matter, so that he could relay the same information back to the controller who was also likely stressing out over not knowing what was happening. (Little did we know there was a mole working for them right in the building, keeping both of them abreast of our daily activity and progress.)

CHAPTER 7

IMPORTANCE OF DOCUMENTATION
(KEEPING TRACK OF THINGS)

Knowing nothing was likely to happen at the division for the rest of the afternoon, I went back to the office I had used for the interviews. It was quiet and secluded, and I knew that I had two things to accomplish.

First, I needed to check in with Tim to determine what he was doing regarding bank accounts, credit card accounts, and other related information. We had confirmation from the interviews that the division used a United Alliance credit card account with multiple cards issued on the account. We didn't have all the credit card statements or supporting charge information, but we had the full account number from the statement provided by the informant. We needed to determine how much volume had been going through that card and for how long.

I also needed Tim to request a search of the banks for any bank accounts we did not have bank statements for. He could start by having the known banks provide a listing of any and all current and past accounts in the name of the division, using the division's federal identification number (or tax identification number) as the identifier of any accounts belonging to the division. Once we had a listing from each bank of all the accounts, we could then compare the records in the boxes to determine if all the statements had been found. One goal was to determine how the United Alliance card had been paid each month.

LEARNING POINT

It is one thing to identify unauthorized, non-business-related personal charges on a company credit card. It is another to determine how the charges were paid. Simply doing one without the other could lead the investigator and the investigation to have problems.

It is not uncommon for a credit card to be paid with multiple checks, one from the business and one from the person who charged personal items on the account. It is also not uncommon for the business to pay 100% of the credit card balance, and have the person who made personal charges provide the business with payment to cover the personal charges. Although paying for the charges doesn't undo the fact that personal charges were made on the account, the fact that the business suffered no financial loss will have an impact on the findings.

When it comes to credit card activity, it is important to determine the following:

1. The business maintained a written policy regarding the permitted uses for the credit card.
2. Individuals with access to the credit cards had knowledge of the policies, including permitted and prohibited uses.
3. Charges on the account were identified and determined to be not business related (i.e., personal in nature).
4. The charges were attributable to an identified individual with access to the credit card in question.
5. Supporting receipts and documentation for the charges identifies that the charges were personal in nature and had no business purpose.
6. The targeted individual did not personally pay for the personal charges, either directly to the credit card company or to the business as reimbursement.
7. The business paid the full amount of the credit card payments, and there were no repayments made personally by the individual to the business to cover the personal expenses.

Second, I needed to catch up on my documentation for the files. My notes in my notebook were good, but more detailed documentation was needed for the files to support the investigation, especially knowing that the results and consequences of these types of investigations were commonly contested by the target, likely leading to civil litigation potentially years down the road. The better and more detailed my documentation was for the files while it was fresh in my mind, the better my recollection would be two or three years down the road when I could be potentially testifying at a trial.

I shut the door and called Tim on his cell phone. He was in his office. I discussed the United Alliance account with him, and he said he had already spoken with customer service at United Alliance, and that they would provide the statements only to the individual named on the account. Tim said they would also provide the statement details if they were provided a valid subpoena or a search warrant. I knew that since a civil or criminal matter had not yet been initiated in this matter, the subpoena and search warrant options were not actual options at this time. That would leave us only the option of a request from the controller himself to United Alliance, or at a minimum, a request signed by the controller to United Alliance for copies of the monthly statements for the account. Tim said he had already started drafting a request to present to the controller to sign, and I indicated I had one from a previous case if needed. I told Tim to make sure the request authorized United Alliance to provide copies of the information directly to Tim. Once drafted, the question that would remain was whether the controller would be willing to sign the request.

I asked Tim where he stood with the division's known bank accounts. Tim said he had all the accounts successfully changed earlier in the day, and that he was now an authorized signer on all the known accounts. I asked Tim if he had already requested a search by each bank for any and all accounts to determine if other accounts existed. Tim said he had already obtained that information, and reviewed the identified accounts to ensure he had been added to each identified account. I asked Tim to provide me with a copy of each bank's listing of accounts, so I could compare the identified accounts to information contained in the boxes.

Tim said he received a voice message from the informant earlier in the day, and that he had spoken with the informant by telephone. Tim said he asked the informant if they knew how the United Alliance account was paid each month. Tim stated the informant said they did not know how the United Alliance account was paid or where the records were stored if they were not found within the office manager's desk along with the bank statements and other paid bills. Tim said the informant also told him that they had spoken with the woman responsible for program-related activities (the woman who admitted to using the card for personal purposes), and that she told the informant that she had been talking with the controller and the office manager each day by telephone. The informant told Tim that the controller and office manager called her at home each night to determine what was happening and both had assured her that they would be cleared of any wrongdoing, that there was nothing to be found, and that they had done nothing wrong or improper.

I finished my call with Tim and reviewed the day's interview notes. I went back through each page of notes, and added further details to each interview not already documented. I added entries for the message left for the office manager requesting to schedule a meeting. When I finished, I went to find the human resource director. She was sitting at the office manager's desk going through the division's mail and invoices. I asked her to come into the office for a minute, and once there, shared with her the information provided by Tim about the woman (a.k.a. "the mole") at the division. I told her we should be careful going forward about what we talk about and where we talked so as to not provide any further information to the controller or office manager through the woman. I also asked her if she thought it made sense to bring her in and ask her more questions, especially directed toward her potential relationship with the controller, the office manager, or both individuals. The human resource director thought we should simply be more careful not to discuss anything at the division, and let the woman continue acting as she has to see what if anything happens with her. I agreed we would wait to talk with her again after we received the United Alliance statements and knew better the extent of her personal activity on the United Alliance account paid by the division.

• • •

I left the division and returned to the main office to continue reviewing the box contents, focusing on looking for how the United Alliance balance was being paid. I also wanted to access the Quick-Books files again, to look for any signs of the United Alliance activity. I found the storage room sealed with the evidence tape intact the way I had last left it. I noted the date and time in my notebook, and broke the seal covering the door. I found the inventory listing and identified the boxes that contained bank statements and supporting information. I carried each box into the designated room, and locked the storage room. I also turned on my computer and accessed the copy of the division's QuickBooks files I had made with the forensic computer specialist prior to returning the computers to the division.

I looked through the chart of accounts (the listing of every account within the QuickBooks company file), the vendor listing (for both active and inactive vendors), the "Other Names" listing (one-time vendors both active and inactive), and the other lists within QuickBooks. I didn't find any activity for United Alliance. Using audit tools and reports available within QuickBooks, I reviewed the voided, changed, and deleted activity to see if the United Alliance activity had been changed or deleted. There was minimal activity and clearly nothing that related to United Alliance payments. It seemed as if the United Alliance activity was never posted by the division within their QuickBooks files.

LEARNING POINT

QuickBooks is a powerful and commonly used accounting package suitable for small- to medium-size businesses and organizations. Accessing information within QuickBooks and generating reports can't be any easier. However, the trade-offs for ease of use and access come in the form of lack of controls over the integrity of the information contained within QuickBooks. Quick-Books is the only accounting package I know that allows users to change or delete transactions after they have already been posted, allowing transactions and information to be easily manipulated. In the hands of an individual committing fraud and seeking concealment of his scheme, QuickBooks easily fits the bill for a desired accounting system. The key to relying on any information generated from QuickBooks is corroboration. Generate the reports, but before relying on them, you need to reconcile them to other information, such as bank statements and canceled checks, to ensure the integrity of the information generated from QuickBooks.

I shut down my laptop and turned my attention to the first box in the room. I emptied the contents on a long table and began sorting the records. The box contained bank statements for several bank accounts at the bank primarily used by the division. Based on the volume of transactions, I determined that at least one of the accounts was the division's primary operating checking account. I started a pile for statements containing that account number, and segregated the other statements and information by account number, resulting in several growing piles on the table. Once I had sorted all the contents into piles, with one pile designated for nonspecific information, I re-sorted the operating statements into sequential order by month and year. I checked through the dates of each statement, and it appeared I had all the monthly statements as far back as the last fiscal year-end, which made sense since the division's files should have been maintained by fiscal year.

Anxious to see if there was any activity relating to United Alliance within the operating account bank statements, I started scanning each month's statement, starting with the earliest month. I scanned the deposits, checks, and electronic withdrawals, looking for any activity with United Alliance. I found nothing in the first month. I continued to the second month, and proceeded month after month until I had reached the end of the stack. There was nothing paid from the operating account to United Alliance during this fiscal year.

Still anxious to see if any payment had ever been made directly from the division's operating account to United Alliance, I found another box that contained financial documents. I put the box contents on a separate table and sorted the contents. I found similar statements for the same bank accounts, but for the last fiscal year. I sorted the operating statements by calendar month, and started reviewing where I had left off, working backwards this time from the latest month to the earliest month. It wasn't until I reached the eighth or ninth statement, which would be within the first few months of the last fiscal year, that I identified an electronic payment made to United Alliance on a statement. I knew a common method to process credit card payments was to have them withdrawn electronically from the bank account, and had a hunch that if I looked long enough I would find activity linking the United Alliance account to a bank account.

The payment was not a large payment, merely a few hundred dollars, not nearly the dollar level I had envisioned based on the information that had been provided by the informant. It was, nonetheless, a payment, and in order for me to link the United Alliance account to a bank account belonging to the division, I needed to find only one transaction. The next question I had was how the bank account could have balanced and reconciled within QuickBooks without the identified transaction on the bank statement.

I retrieved my laptop and booted it again, expecting to find one of two things. Either the account was not balanced and reconciled within QuickBooks as thought, or a transaction had to have been entered into QuickBooks using different information from the United Alliance payment, allowing the account to balance and reconcile. Once I was back into the division's QuickBooks file, I scrolled through the operating account register to the date of the payment on the bank statement. Sure enough there was a posted transaction in the register for the same date and the same dollar amount. However, rather than being a payment to United Alliance, the transaction was posted as a general journal entry. The entry included the following description, "Draw—Controller's Name." The entry and amount was posted to the "Office Expense" account. I scanned the rest of the register of the operating account for similar entries. None were found. I printed the general journal entry and placed it into a clear sleeve, then attached an evidence sticker to the sleeve. I labeled the evidence sticker with the date, time, location, and description, and placed the sleeve with the boxes.

Having found the first sign of activity relating to the United Alliance account being concealed from detection, I realized the lateness of the day and decided to end on that note. I put the organized bank records back into each respective box, and brought the boxes back to the storage room. Once all the boxes were inside, I locked the door and sealed it with evidence tape. I noted the date and time in my notebook, then returned to the room to make more notes on my findings. I decided I would sit on the latest findings until tomorrow, after I had spent more time going through the bank statements and information in the boxes.

● ● ●

At home that evening, I revisited my notebook and read through the day's notes. I added more details and described how I had found the payment to United Alliance on the bank statement, as well as the concealed United Alliance payment within QuickBooks.

The next morning I returned to the boxes. I met the senior accountant and brought him up to speed with my previous day's findings. I left the senior accountant with the boxes and found Tim. I reviewed the various bank accounts identified by each bank with him. I changed my mind about waiting, and shared with him the concealed United Alliance payment. Tim seemed pleased that pieces of the puzzle were starting to come together. I asked Tim where he stood with the request for the controller to sign for the United Alliance statements, and he said the request was finished and forwarded to counsel for review and approval. Tim said that once the request was approved, he would contact the controller to set up a date and time to discuss the financial analysis of the division.

I returned to the senior accountant and went to work with the bank account listings and boxes of evidence. I retrieved the boxes from the storage room, noting the date and time I broke the seal on the door. I put the piles back out on the tables from yesterday, and started to match up the bank statements with the listed bank accounts. I retrieved more boxes containing financial information and sorted through the contents, putting any bank accounting information into stacks on still more tables to ensure I kept each box's contents separate. It became apparent that the division maintained far too many bank accounts, and as an aside I made a note to recommend the division consolidate the bank accounts into a minimal number of accounts.

LEARNING POINT

By now you should have noticed that I never left the collected evidence alone or unattended for any time. In order to ensure the chain of custody (discussed earlier) remains intact, protecting the admissibility of the evidence, the evidence needs to remain secured at all times until presented in court. In the event the evidence needs to be removed from a secured storage location, it must be attended at all times, and never left alone in a room, let alone in a car. Properly maintain chain-of-custody accounts for the evidence's movements, from the time it is collected to the time it is presented in court.

Working with the senior accountant, it wasn't until later in the day that we were able to match all the piles to the listed bank accounts, and identify the accounts that we had not found any information for. As we found information pertaining to each bank account, we found the same account on the lists provided by the banks and highlighted the listed account in yellow. As I scanned the lists for any accounts that were not highlighted, I saw one account that was provided on the list that was labeled *closed*. The listing indicated the account was closed three months earlier.

I wanted to know why I didn't find any bank statements or other information for this account, so I left the senior accountant with the boxes and brought the listing to Tim. Tim indicated the identified account was included with all the other accounts for which Tim had already requested monthly statements. Knowing that it could take up to 12 weeks for the bank to produce the requested statements, I asked Tim to make a special request of the bank for that one particular bank account, to see if we could get access to the bank statements sooner. Tim said he would go over to the bank and see what they would do for him for that one account.

● ● ●

When I returned back to the boxes, the senior accountant indicated the human resource director had called looking for me. He said she was out at the division, and that I was to call her once I received the message. I went to the phone in the corner of the room and called her.

The human resource director told me that the office manager called the division returning my message, and provided me with a phone number where I could reach him. I asked her if there was any substance to her conversation with the office manager, and she said there was no conversation.

I hung up with her and called the number she provided. A male answered, and I asked if I had reached the office manager. He asked who was calling, and I told him my name. I asked him if we could set up a time to meet to discuss the financial aspects of the division. He asked me if he had to meet with me. I told him he didn't have to do anything, but also reminded him that he was still an employee on paid administrative leave, and that if he did not meet with me, I would forward that information to the human resource director. He asked me what we would talk about. I told him we would discuss the financial operations and bookkeeping procedures of the division, as well as the roles and responsibilities of the individuals who worked within the division. He asked me where we would meet, and I told him we should meet out at the division, so that if there was any information he needed to get regarding the division, he would have access to it (he likely didn't know the extent to which we had removed the financial documentation from the division, as the mole didn't have access to those areas and no one was present when we removed all the documents that first day).

He agreed to meet, and asked when I wanted to meet. I suggested we meet tomorrow morning, 9:00 A.M., as I already had something to do today in the afternoon (and I knew I wanted to ensure we had an entire day to meet if needed without running out of time in the event he had to be somewhere today). I really didn't have anything in the afternoon, but he had no way of knowing that, and I wanted time to prepare for the interview. I also wanted to keep the office manager in suspense a bit longer, rather than satisfy his need for knowledge on the same day he called and spoke with me. Anxiety is a good thing.

He agreed to meet, and we scheduled our meeting for the next day, first thing in the morning at the division. He hung up and I retrieved my notebook to document the call. Then, I shared the call with the senior accountant who had heard most of it anyway because he was in the same room with me. I called the human resource director, and asked that she come back to the division to meet me early tomorrow morning to let me in, as well as to act as a witness if needed during the interview. She said she would be out there anyway making a deposit and going through the bills to be paid by the division.

I left the senior accountant with the boxes and went to find Tim. I stood in his doorway while he finished a call, and sat down in front of his desk after he waved me in. Once he finished the call I told him I had just spoken with the office manager, and that I would be meeting him in the morning.

• • •

Without the bank records for the identified account and the United Alliance statements, I turned my attention to preparing for tomorrow's interview with the office manager. I returned to the senior accountant, and together we put the records back into the boxes. Once we returned all the boxes to the storage room, I sealed the room again, noting the date and time in my notes. The senior accountant went off to work on other things and I returned to my notebook to review my notes from my initial interaction with the office manager.

I spent the rest of the afternoon preparing an outline and notes of issues I wanted to discuss with the office manager. The three most important questions I had to resolve were as follows:

1. How much activity went through the United Alliance account and for how long?
2. How was the United Alliance account paid each month?
3. Where did the funds come from to pay the United Alliance account?

I listed out the areas where the office manager had provided inaccurate, misleading, or outright deceptive responses during our interview on the first day. Things like no credit card and no new bank accounts. I wanted to see if he would tell me what his relationship was with the controller, as well as the women in the office, including the woman who worked right alongside him and cried all the time, and the woman who charged personal activity on the United Alliance card (a.k.a. the mole). I also wanted to determine what else may have been happening at the division beyond the United Alliance account. It is not unusual for interviewees to provide knowledge of other fraudulent or illegal activity, especially if it is perceived to take the focus and heat off of them (at least for a little while).

LEARNING POINT

To ensure an effective interview, you must prepare in advance for the interview, provided the interview wasn't needed to be conducted on a spontaneous basis, which is rarely the case. Identifying the areas that need to be covered, questions to be asked, and issues to be resolved will help ensure nothing is missed due to a lack of memory. The entire interview doesn't need to be written out, but a general outline will help ensure all areas are covered prior to ending the interview. In many cases, you will only get one chance at an interview, so best to plan as if each interview will be the only interview that will be conducted.

Planning should also encompass the physical environment and details for the interview, as discussed earlier and below.

As I thought about the upcoming interview in the morning, I called the human resource director to see if she was going to be out at the division until the end of the day. I wanted to walk through the space and offices again with this interview in mind, and select the most appropriate location to have the meeting. She answered and indicated she would wait for me to come out. I finished making notes on what I wanted to accomplish and headed out to the division.

I arrived at the division to find the human resource director working at the office manager's desk, reviewing the mail and sorting bills to be paid just as she said she would be doing. We talked about my call with the office manager for a few minutes, and then I walked through the division looking at each office. The office I had used to conduct the interviews with the other employees was good for that purpose, quiet and secluded, but it was a distance from the office manager's desk. I was concerned about being that far away should the interview not go well. I wanted a space that was private, yet close enough to the human resource director. It had to be away from his work area where he could find comfort if he became stressed, and yet include no distractions. I decided on the office immediately adjacent to the office manager's desk. The human resource director could work right at his desk just outside the office, and if needed, could come in within seconds. I also figured with her working right outside the office, she would be able to hear everything said during the interview (my hunch was proved to be correct after the interview was finished). I sat at the table and determined where I would sit as well as where I would have the office manager sit. I then sat in the seat I identified for the office manager, and looked around the office for any distractions potentially available to him. I moved things from in front of where he would be sitting to shelves behind him. Other things were moved into boxes and put away, leaving as little as possible in the office.

Once I thought I was finished, I asked the human resource director to come in. I had her sit in the chair identified for the office manager, and asked her what she thought were distractions. I moved everything she identified. Then, I sat in my seat and thought about the office manager sitting across the table from me. I asked the human resource director a few questions, and looked to see if I had any distractions that could take my attention from the office manager. All the things I had moved behind the office manager's seat needed to be moved again, as I could see myself looking up at them while listening to the office manager (I was looking at them already while listening to the human resource director).

I had the human resource director return to the office manager's desk, and asked her to listen to me while I talked on my cell phone. I closed the door and called a friend. I talked at a normal tone with my friend for a minute or two, and then I went out to ask the human resource director if she had heard what I was saying. She had heard everything, and I wasn't speaking loudly on my phone.

With the office chosen and set for the morning's interview, I turned off the lights and grabbed my things to leave. I asked the human resource director to meet me in the morning at the division at 8:15 A.M., to provide me with a solid half-hour of preparation time prior to the interview. I asked her to be prepared to come into the interview if needed, especially if the office manager confessed or provided some information that could immediately impact the current employment status (paid administrative leave) of any individuals.

LEARNING POINT

Planning for an interview should also encompass how to document the interview, having supplies on hand such as a pad and pen, and considering "what-if" scenarios. For instance, what if the interviewee admits to some wrongdoing during the interview? Are you prepared to have the interviewee write out in detail his story? Will someone be available if needed to witness and/or notarize his written statement if one is provided? What happens if the individual admits to wrongdoing, and the plan is to place the individual on paid administrative leave pending a decision on his fate with the organization? Will someone appropriate with human resources responsibilities be available to place the individual on leave? Once the interview has begun, it may be too late to have these issues addressed on the spot. The best-case scenario is to have contemplated these types of issues in advance, and if needed, execute the plan. The worst-case scenario is that resources are prepared to act, but end up never needing to react.

She said she would be working right outside the office and would hear everything. She said she could be in the meeting within seconds if there became such a need. I thanked her and headed out the door. It was the end of another long day.

CHAPTER 8

FURTHER INVESTIGATIVE MEASURES
(OBTAINING MORE EVIDENCE)

I didn't sleep all that well that night. I thought about the upcoming interview, the things that I hoped went well, and potential problems or issues I could face. I tried to remember everything about the office manager from the first day. He was a young guy, still living at home with his parents from what I was told, and could be a potentially angry person having been abruptly removed from his job and placed on leave (albeit paid leave, so a vacation in essence). I still didn't know much regarding the level of potential fraud I could be facing at the division. I didn't know if he would do anything rash or behave irrationally in a desperate attempt to derail the investigation. And I didn't know if he could become hostile. I knew the mole was keeping him informed until we stopped talking around her, and that there had to be some kind of need for information he was experiencing that no longer was being fulfilled. One thing I did know was that the information he had provided me with on the first day was not accurate and was likely grounds for termination of employment, in and of itself, for lying when questioned about employment-related matters.

The potential for a bad situation was ever present, and I thought about my safety, as well as the safety of the human resource director. I had checked the day before and I knew the women of the division would not be in tomorrow morning, leaving the place to ourselves for the interview. I thought about the need to determine what the office manager knew, especially if he provided anything that could lead us to the information faster than the measures we already had in place. I decided the meeting would occur as planned, but if anger, hostility, or other risks became obvious, I would immediately end the meeting and set a time to continue the conversation, allowing time to cool off, as well as raise the safety measures to a more appropriate level.

There was also the strong chance that he wouldn't show up for the meeting at all, or would call at the last minute to cancel due to "an unexpected change or urgent need or something." Based on what I knew thus far, the office manager was told we were at the division to conduct a financial review and as part of that review I would need to speak with the employees. Aside from being paid to stay home, there was no reason for the office manager to cause us harm. If he wanted to end the meeting and leave, I would let him, and then he would likely be placed on unpaid leave for insubordination for his lack of cooperation with the financial review.

LEARNING POINT

It is common to set up these meetings and interviews, only to have them canceled, delayed, or have a no-show. Sudden illnesses and last-minute cancelations are frequent, especially when the target of an investigation knows he may finally have to discuss details of his scheme that he has been concealing for some time. Having to admit to wrongdoing creates much stress, and it is human nature to delay that confrontation as long as possible. Fight or flight? In my experience the target will choose flight. Rather than get annoyed or take it personally, you need to accept the fact that delays and cancellations are just part of the process. Rescheduling even at the last minute to accommodate a scheduling issue with the target is one thing, but in each case a decision will need to be made as to how long you will wait, and how many times you will reschedule the meeting, simply to accommodate the interviewee. At some point you may need to pull the plug on conducting the interview, simply document the meeting attempts, delays, and cancellations, and complete the investigation without the interview. The fact that you tried on several occasions to meet with the individual to get the facts from his perspective and to discuss your findings will only show that you attempted to be thorough with your procedures. In the end, if additional facts later become known through the individual that could change your conclusion, you will be able to show that you attempted to get that information from the individual prior to completing your work and drafting your report.

I headed out to the division, running through the interview in my mind. It seemed like the shortest ride yet. I arrived to find the human resource director waiting for me in the lobby. Having just arrived herself, she was still turning on the lights and things. The weather was noticeably pleasant, and it was only going to get warmer as the day progressed. I was wearing my khaki pants and a polo shirt—short sleeves, because it was going to be warm in the afternoon. I asked her if she thought the office manager would show up today, and she said she thought he would not show for the meeting. I bet her a dollar that he would show. I went into the office to make sure everything was as I had left it and put my notes on the table.

• • •

As it got closer to 9:00, we stood in the lobby and looked out the front windows to see if he would show up. If he parked around the corner and walked up, we wouldn't see him until he crossed the front walkway and headed toward the front door. We both thought he would park right out in front, and that we would see him as he pulled up. Just before 9:00, a shiny, new, luxury four-door sedan pulled up across the street and stopped. As the door opened, we both recognized the driver as the office manager. The funny thing was we knew he drove an older Ford Bronco and only made $28,000 a year working at the division, so the car was obviously not his, nor was it consistent with his lifestyle still living at home with his parents. The car was likely his parents' car, but we were unsure what his message was in coming in their expensive car. When he stood up outside the car, we instantly noticed the full-length leather coat he was wearing. One of the warmest days so far this season and forecasted to only get warmer, and the office manager drives over in an expensive new car wearing a full-length leather coat.

I looked at the human resource director and said I had one very important question to get answered before we proceeded. What was under that long leather coat? My mind raced as I tried to find a way to determine if there could be a weapon hidden below the long coat. Then the idea popped into my head. It would work, but only if the office manager wasn't too bright—something I was banking on. I ran back into the office where we were to meet and cranked the thermostat as high as possible. Then, I opened a window in the room, and returned back to the lobby. I didn't want to leave the human resource manager alone when he came through the door.

He opened the exterior door and knocked. I looked at the human resource director and said "Here we go." I opened the door. I immediately stuck out my right hand to shake his hand, and thanked him for coming in to meet with me. He didn't seem fazed and shook my hand. Then the human resource director re-introduced herself to him and thanked him for coming in. I watched him as he scanned the lobby and areas. Then I asked him to come in. As we walked down the hallway toward his desk, I told him that we would be meeting in the office just beyond his desk. I then asked him if that would be a good place to meet. His response was "whatever." Then I told him there was one other thing. I told him that the thermostats in the back had been malfunctioning during the week, and that the offices got extremely hot throughout the day, causing us to open windows at times. I asked him if that had ever happened while he was there. He said not that he was aware (and wouldn't he be aware of it, since he worked just outside the office we were about to meet in, every day for how long?). I said to him that I thought it would be a lot more comfortable given the heat situation if he left his coat outside on the chair right near the door, because it was only going to get hotter when we closed the door. Unfazed, he agreed and took that long, potentially weapon-concealing leather coat off in front of the human resource director, and laid it on the chair. What he didn't realize was that I was scanning him the entire time to ensure there were no weapons hidden under his coat. Now with his coat off, I could see around his waist—no bulges. That's not to say he couldn't have something hidden elsewhere on his body, but at least I wasn't going to be distracted wondering and worrying constantly about what might be looming under his coat.

I was so thankful he wasn't brighter than he turned out to be. I was wearing short sleeves, the window was already opened, and we could have simply left the door open during the meeting, reducing the risk of the office getting too warm, which would have allowed him to keep the coat on. Needless to say I was relieved.

I directed him to his seat, and went over to where I planned on sitting. He sat down, and then I followed. I started by apologizing for the abrupt way we had met just a few days earlier. I told him it wasn't my call to complete the financial review in that fashion, but just as he took direction from others, I did from my client. I asked him what he remembered from our first encounter. He said he remembered us bursting into the division, and bringing him and the others into the office while members of our team started going through everything. The next thing he remembered was being escorted out of the office like some criminal, and walking out the front door. He seemed a bit angry, but not hostile.

I asked him if he remembered speaking with me and any of the questions I asked him that day. He said he remembered talking to me, but couldn't recall what we talked about. He said it all happened so fast, he wasn't sure if he even provided accurate answers to the questions asked. I thought this was a nice defense he had created in the event that I showed him the information he provided was less than accurate.

I thought I would start with some basic foundational questions, relatively harmless and totally nonthreatening, and asked him to describe what he did at the division. His reply was that he did everything. I said to him that we needed to get a little more specific. I then asked him to describe his original duties and responsibilities when he first started at the division, and if they evolved or changed over time, and to describe how and when they changed. He asked me what I meant. I asked him to identify the main things he did on a day-to-day basis. He said he made deposits, paid bills, and managed the finances for the division. There it was—short and sweet, and to the point. I asked him what making the deposits entailed. He said he took the money that came in, recorded it into the system, and brought it to the bank. He said that's what you do when you make deposits. I thought to myself, "Either this guy is an idiot, or he thinks I am an idiot." Either way, I knew I should delve a bit further to see why his responses to these innocuous questions were so bizarre.

• • •

I asked him to describe how money came into the division. He said funds came in, and they got recorded. I asked him how funds came in, and he said he didn't understand my question. I asked him to describe the different ways funds were received into the division. He said either they were brought in or they were mailed in. I asked him what form the funds were in when they were received. Again, he said he didn't understand my question. I asked him if they paid by cash, check, credit card, and/or other means of payment. He said they paid in all of those forms. I asked him who handled the payments when they were mailed into the division. He said the woman sitting near his desk (a.k.a. the crier) handled all the payments and wrote out receipts for the payments she received. I asked him what happened to the funds after the woman received them. He said she put the funds into the safe at the end of each day. I asked him who had access to the safe. He said he didn't understand my question. I asked him who had the combination or key to get into the safe where the funds were placed by the woman. He said the controller had access to the safe. I asked him if anyone else had access to the safe. He said the woman had access, but it was kept open during the day so that she could put the money into the safe at the end of each day. I asked him if anyone else had access, meaning the ability to open the locked safe. He said he could open the safe, if needed. I asked him if the woman could open the safe if it was closed. He said she couldn't open the safe, but that it was always open for her to use. I asked him how often he opened the safe. He said he just told me that it was always open during the day for anyone including himself to use, if needed. I said I heard what he said, but my question was how often did you have to unlock the safe and open it for the day? He said he didn't understand what I was asking.

I thought to myself, "No one is that ignorant." The office manager was clearly playing games with his responses, and likely thought his cute responses and selective memory would prevent him from divulging any information potentially implicating him in any wrongdoing. This seemed to be consistent with what he told the informant—that he would be cleared of any wrongdoing and shown to have done nothing wrong.

LEARNING POINT

While not holding myself out as an expert in interviewing techniques, I have had great experience in getting individuals to meet, talk, and admit to their actions, even when they didn't want to provide any information. In my experience, people react in strange ways to stress, and having these types

(Continued)

of meetings can be very stressful to the target. Some people get nervous and quiet, while others can get hostile toward the interviewer. Expect the unexpected, and never let your guard down. In this case the individual clearly chose to play dumb, in a poor attempt to show me how smart he was by not providing any responses or information. As with delays and cancellations, it is important not to get frustrated or let people's behavior and responses (or lack thereof) personally affect you during these interviews. By not reacting to their comments and behavior, and by maintaining your composure throughout the meeting, you are more likely to accomplish your objectives and identify information they provide even when they think they are providing you no information.

I continued along the same line of questions and answers regarding the paying of bills and other financial duties. Each line of questioning followed the same course. First, there was the lack of understanding, and then in response to my asking each question a different way, his answers were vague and uninformative. We played the back-and-forth game for a half-hour or so, and then I decided to turn the heat up a bit on the interview.

I asked him if he remembered his response when I asked him about any new bank accounts. He said he couldn't recall. I said he told me that there were no new bank accounts. He said he must have misunderstood what I was asking at the time, because there was an account that was opened just before that day but that there was next to no activity in the account because it was so new. He said he didn't think about that account because it had just been opened and there was little or no activity in it. I asked him what he thought I meant when I originally asked him if the division had opened any new accounts recently. He said he didn't think I meant accounts that didn't have activity in them.

I thought to myself, "The mole obviously knew and told him that we had found the bank information about the new account that he had opened, and therefore he had ample time to prepare an explanation." I knew he wasn't smart enough to have remembered what was in his trash pail when we showed up the first day.

I asked him why the account was opened in the first place. He said the controller told him to open a new account so he did. I asked him why the controller wanted a new account opened. He said I should ask the controller that question. I asked him what he knew about the purpose or use for the new bank account. He said he had just told me to ask the controller why he wanted the new account.

I asked him why an existing bank account had been closed recently. He said the controller told him to close out the account, and so he did. I asked him what the account had been previously used for. He said the controller mainly used the account, and that I should ask the controller about the closed account. I asked him if he maintained any records about the closed account. He said the account was maintained by the controller, and that I should ask him those questions. I asked him where the records were for that account. He said he just told me to ask the controller about the account. I asked him if he ever had any access to the account, or reconciled the account, or recorded the activity of the account. He said no.

I knew from the mailing address on the statements found and the fact that all the bank-related information was found in his desk that he likely received the bank statement each month for this account as well, reviewed and reconciled it somewhere off the division's books, and that he knew exactly what the account activity and history entailed.

I asked him how money went into the bank account. He said there were deposits made into the account by the controller. I asked him the nature or source of the deposits. He said that I should ask the controller that question, as he didn't have any involvement with the account. I asked him if he ever made any transactions with the bank account. He said no, that the controller handled that account. I asked him into what bank account the payments received by the woman were deposited. He said those funds were deposited into the operating checking account. I asked him about payments that were received in the mail. He said the mail went to the same woman, and that she would include payments received in the mail with the other payments she received in person. I asked him if all the payments received were provided a written receipt. He said that that was the way it was supposed to work. I asked him if that was the actual way it worked. He said he believed it was, but that I should ask the woman that question. I asked him who handled the payments when the woman was out of the office, on vacation, or at lunch. He said he would handle the payments. I asked him if he followed the procedures and wrote out a receipt. He said he did. I asked him where the receipt books were maintained. He said everything should have been right in his desk drawers for the current year, and in the boxes for the prior years.

I remembered that I saw maybe one manual receipt book within the contents of all the boxes we had collected and stored. The question that remained was where were all the receipt books if a written receipt was written for every payment received?

I asked him to describe how it worked if a payment was received by credit card. He said they processed the charge. I asked him if they came in person, or if they mailed in their card information. He said both. I asked him who physically entered the charge into the credit card terminal and processed the charge to the member's card. He said the woman processed the cards. I asked him who handled the credit card payments when she was away or unavailable. He said he processed the cards. I asked him if anyone else had access to process credit card transactions. He said anyone who walked up to the credit card terminal could process a transaction. I asked him what he did when he processed a charge. He said he swiped the card, entered the amount, printed the slips, had the member sign the slip, and left the slip for the woman on her desk. I asked him if he wrote out a receipt for credit card payments. He said no, because the credit card slip was the member's receipt. I asked him if he wrote out a receipt when a member paid by check. He said no because their canceled check was their receipt. I said then, "The only time you wrote out a receipt was when cash was received." He said, "Basically." I asked "What do you mean, 'Basically'?" I asked him at what other time did a receipt get written for a payment. He said never. I said, "Then the only time a receipt was provided was when cash was received?" He had no further response.

• • •

I was starting to get an idea of how the account was likely funded, and how the credit card was likely being paid (through the "controller's" bank account). I wanted to see just how much he was willing to provide me regarding the likely scheme, or at least this likely scheme. There could also be other schemes yet to be identified—the interview was far from over.

I asked him if the credit card terminal was closed and reconciled on a regular basis to the bank deposits and bookkeeping system (QuickBooks), such as on a daily basis at the end of each day. He said it wasn't used that way. I asked him to describe how it was used. He said he just finished describing how it was used. I asked him to explain how the credit card activity was reconciled to the bank statement and accounting transactions. He said he recorded the credit card activity by general journal entry after each deposit made into the account. He said the credit card activity was just part of the entry made. I asked him if anyone else made entries into QuickBooks or any other bookkeeping records. He said no. I asked him who handled those responsibilities when he was away or out. He said he has never been away or out, and no one handled the QuickBooks.

I thought to myself, "That was a good response in light of the United Alliance payment entered into QuickBooks under a different description." In his own words, he had just told me that no one else entered activity into their QuickBooks.

LEARNING POINT

During the interview, asking the right questions will yield the most information. Done properly, you can get people to provide information that you may be able to use against them. Often they will provide information you didn't know or expect, expanding the case. In my experience I have found that if I can get individuals to describe how something was supposed to work, and also how it actually worked, I can use their descriptions to expand the interview. By "playing dumb" and asking a lot of questions, you allow the interviewee to provide as many rich details as possible, even though you likely have a good, detailed understanding of how it worked through procedures performed prior to the interview. You can use this nonthreatening discussion to calibrate the individual and his body language, and watch for changes as you move into discussions about his actions and involvement.

In this case I got the office manager to describe the bookkeeping and accounting in his own words, as well as who had access and ability to record transactions within QuickBooks. He stated no one else had access. Then he stated he made all the entries within QuickBooks. When I asked him about questionable transactions and discrepancies within QuickBooks, he stated he didn't know. I reminded him that he just told me he had the only access to QuickBooks, and that only he entered information into QuickBooks, and

(Continued)

therefore he should know the answer to my question. Then I asked him who else could have entered the activity, and proceeded down that line of questioning.

The key in this interview was to get the interviewee to provide foundational information and continue to build upon that foundation, setting the stage to show that he and only he was responsible for the activity (in QuickBooks in this case).

Having spent a good half-hour talking only about the payments received into the division, I turned my attention to expenses and bills of the division. I asked the office manager to describe the typical expenses incurred by the division. He said utilities, oil, security, payroll, supplies, and those kinds of things. I asked him to describe the process of paying bills at the division. He said he didn't understand the question. I asked him to walk me through how a bill is received and ultimately processed for payment and filed. He said the bills came in, he wrote the checks, and the controller signed the checks. I asked him if any signature stamps existed. He said there was one stamp. I asked him whose signature was on the stamp. He said it was the controller's signature. I asked him who handled the signature stamp. He said that he maintained the signature stamp so that no one else could get unauthorized access to the stamp. I asked him where the division's blank checks were maintained. He said they were kept in the drawer below the printer. I asked him if the drawer was locked. He said the drawer was never locked.

I realized I had just identified another potential way funds could have been diverted from the division. Checks could have been written and stamped with the signature stamp by the controller. The statements likely came in and went directly to the office manager for reconciling, and it was likely to be found that the controller never looked at the bank statements or reconciliations. I noted it was something to look further into after the interview. I asked him more questions about how expenses were incurred, approved, selected for payment, and ultimately paid to the vendors.

I next asked him to describe the payroll process. He said the employees' hours were called in, and the next day a package arrived with their paychecks and reports. I asked him who called in their hours. He said he called in the hours. I asked him who received and opened the payroll information when it was received the next day. He said he received and opened the payroll, and used the reports to record the payroll within QuickBooks. I asked him who else reviewed the payroll reports and information. He said no one. I asked him if he had ever seen anything unusual or unexpected within a payroll batch received. He said he didn't understand my question. I asked him if he recognized anyone getting paid when they weren't supposed to, or anything like that. He said he never saw anything unusual. I asked him more questions about how employees were paid and how much each person made at the division.

I already knew the human resource director had requested copies of the employees' W-2s and the year-to-date payroll report directly from the payroll provider, and having already received them, was able to tell me she didn't see anything suspicious in the amounts and transactions within the reports.

• • •

I looked at the clock. We had been meeting for nearly two hours. He looked at the clock as well, and then he rolled up his right sleeve and looked down at his watch. He asked me how much longer I thought we would need to meet, and that he had someplace to be. I asked him what time he needed to be somewhere. He said it didn't matter.

Knowing that he was getting impatient, and not knowing how long he would tolerate my questions, I decided to head right for the most important information. I asked him if he remembered his response regarding credit cards used by the division. He said he told me there were no cards presently in use by the division. I asked him if he remembered a United Alliance account. He said the division had an account at one time, but that the United Alliance account was closed at the time I asked him the question, and therefore the division had no credit cards. I asked him if there were any other credit card accounts other than the closed United Alliance account. He said not to his knowledge. I asked him, if there were any other cards, wouldn't he be aware of them, as he paid all the bills and received all the statements? He said not that he was aware of. I asked him if he ever used the United Alliance card. He said he had used it twice. The first time was in making a purchase for the office under the direction of the controller, and the second time was in paying the bill for a meeting held with the controller. He said he didn't want to use the card that day, but the controller told him to put the invoice on the card. I asked him if he had ever used the card for personal purposes. He said no. I asked him if anyone else ever used the card for personal purchases. He said the program manager (the woman with the card) used it with the approval of the controller, and that I should ask them about her use of the card. I asked him if she ever reimbursed the division for her use of the card. He said not that he was aware of, and that I should ask them about that. I asked him, if he was the person responsible for making the deposits and recording the bookkeeping, wouldn't he be aware of any repayments by the individual? He told me to ask the controller about that.

I asked him who received the statement in the mail each month. He said it went to the controller. I asked him if he ever reviewed or reconciled the statements. He said no. I asked him how the United Alliance account was paid each month. He told me to ask the controller about that. I said that I thought he was responsible for paying all the invoices and bills for the division, and as such he should have been aware of how the United Alliance account was being paid. He said the controller handled all aspects of the United Alliance account and how it was paid, and that I needed to talk with the controller about it.

I asked him if he thought anyone at the division was stealing funds from the organization. He said he didn't understand the question. I said to him that he was the person primarily responsible for the receipts, deposits, purchases, disbursements, and payroll, and that if anyone would be aware of funds being diverted or used for personal purposes, it would be him. He said he wasn't aware of anyone stealing from the division, but that others were also involved in making the deposits and paying the bills, and that maybe someone else may know of something. I asked him why the United Alliance payment identified on the operating bank statement was entered into QuickBooks with different information. He said he never entered any United Alliance activity into QuickBooks, and that he never had the statements to enter the activity. I asked him if there were any other transactions posted within QuickBooks that were different from the underlying transactions. He said he didn't understand my question.

He began to look at the clock and his watch again. He was slouched down a bit in his chair, and I could tell he was anxious to end the meeting. In an attempt to lighten things up for him, I asked him what he did in the off time when he wasn't working at the division (I already knew he belonged to several clubs and acted as the treasurer of at least one of them). That question pressed a nerve. He sat right up and turned bright red. He said what he did on his personal time was none of my business, and had nothing to do with his responsibilities at the division. He seemed pretty agitated. I said I was simply trying to learn more about the person I was talking with, to be more social than "Just the facts, ma'am." He repeated that what he did was none of my business.

I asked him if there was anything he wanted to add to the information he provided. He said there was nothing else, and that we had talked about everything. I asked him, if he had any of the division's records or items at his house or in his car. He said he had nothing that belonged to the division. I asked him, if we needed to meet again, would he be willing to come back to discuss things further? He said that would be fine, and stood up to leave the room. I stood up, and walked to the door to open it, allowing him to leave and allowing me to observe him at all times.

He walked out of the office, picked up his long leather coat, and headed straight toward the front door. I walked behind him, and as we walked down the hall, I thanked him for coming in and spending the time with me. He didn't respond, opened the front door, and walked out straight down the front walk. I shut the door behind him, ensuring it was locked so that he couldn't simply return, and stood next to the human resource director as we watched him cross the street and get back into the shiny black car. He drove away, and we continued to watch for a few minutes to ensure he didn't circle and come back.

● ● ●

I needed a break. I asked the human resource director if she heard our conversation. She said she heard more than 90 percent of what was discussed. She also said she took notes based on what she heard, and that she didn't think she missed anything of importance. I asked her what she thought of the meeting and his responses. She said he obviously knew about the bank account and the United Alliance account, and was likely aware of other things happening at the division. I asked her what her thoughts were on continuing his employment on paid administrative leave status. She said the fact that he lied to us on the first day, and failed to respond completely and appropriately today to my questions was likely sufficient grounds to terminate his employment. She asked me if I thought I was going to get any further information or cooperation from him to resolve this matter. I told her that he was not likely to provide anything further, and that his sole motive for today's meeting was likely to learn what we knew to date to share with the controller. She said that even if he wasn't terminated right away, he was going to be changed to unpaid administrative leave once she spoke with outside counsel and documented his file.

To me it seemed pretty straightforward. The office manager was primarily responsible for the accounting and bookkeeping of the division, and as such, he had firsthand knowledge of things that were happening. He admitted to opening the bank account, only to lie about it on the first day. He said he was the person who entered the activity into QuickBooks, and that no one else entered activity into QuickBooks. He admitted he knew about the United Alliance account, and that at least one unauthorized individual was using the card for personal purposes. Yet he didn't do anything or tell anyone at the main office about these things.

The human resource director walked back to the desk where she was working to call outside counsel and discuss what to do with the office manager. I returned to the room where I had met with the office manager, retrieved my notebook, and began documenting as much of the interview as possible, filling in details around the notes I had taken.

LEARNING POINT

While it is important to memorialize a meeting or interview, consideration must be made as to how that will be accomplished. Most fraud examiners outside of law enforcement lack interview rooms equipped with two-way windows, video, and other recording technology. Video or electronic recording of a meeting or interview often creates a potential barrier to free-flowing

(Continued)

(Continued)

information from the target, causing him to respond cautiously or in a reserved manner. I know personally I would be more careful what I would say if I knew I was being recorded, and so I would expect anyone else would behave similarly.

Taking notes is important during an interview, but if you spend your time writing down every last word people said, two things will likely occur. First, by taking copious notes, you likely spent much of the time looking down at your notes versus watching the individual and his reactions to questions. Body language is often more important than their verbal responses. Second, note taking also creates a barrier, as the interviewee will be talking and watching you write things down that he said.

Consider having a second person at the meeting or interview who can take notes and make observations, allowing you to focus on talking with the target while observing all his body language without any distraction.

FRAUD FACTS

Body language is the nonverbal or unspoken mode of communication and interaction. It involves gestures, mannerisms, and other bodily signs. Body language is like a mirror that informs you of the thoughts and feelings of the other person in response to words and actions.

How important is learning how to read and use body language?

- 8% of the information we receive is from what people actually say.
- 37% of information we receive is from their tone, inflection, and speed of their voice.
- A staggering 55% of the information we receive is from their body language.

Different signals contribute to different meanings depending on the individual and scenario. A guide is to look for three or four signals that share the same meaning.[1]

I knew Tim was anxiously waiting to hear how the meeting went, so I went down to the private office I used to interview other employees and called him. I knew other employees could be coming into the division at some time during the day, and I wanted to be sure no one, including our mole, heard any of the conversation. I thought it was likely the office manager had already called the controller to fill him in on the morning meeting, likely from his cell phone while driving away from the division. I was also sure the office manager would be talking with the others as he had in the past, if he hadn't done so already.

I called Tim and provided him a five-minute rundown of the interview, especially the long leather coat. That's when I remembered the heat was still cranked up in the area where we met. I scratched a note to remind myself to walk down and turn off the heat. Tim seemed pleased with the findings. He asked if I thought we had enough from the meeting to contemplate having the office manager charged as a conspirator should criminal charges be pursued. I told Tim I thought the office manager should be terminated for now, and as the case was further investigated and additional evidence was found, a determination could be made regarding the extent the office manager may have been involved in any schemes. I said I thought, based on how the office manager acted and responded, that he likely had some scheme of his own being perpetrated beyond the bank account and United Alliance account, both areas he clearly attempted to distance himself from.

I asked Tim where he stood with receiving the bank statements for the identified bank account. He said he had spoken with the bank earlier, and that the statements would be available for him to pick up by the end of the week. I thought that was pretty fast service from the bank based on my personal experience, but I also knew the organization's relationship with the bank was very important to the bank, so I wasn't all that surprised with their prompt attention to his request.

As I was finishing my call with Tim, there was a knock on the door. I asked Tim to hold for a moment while I saw who was knocking, and I set the phone down. I opened the door and an individual I had yet to meet was standing at the door. She introduced herself by providing her name, and then stated she was the informant providing information to Tim. I asked her to come in, and I shut the door behind her. I went back to the phone and told Tim that an individual who identified herself as the informant just came into the office. Tim said he knew that she would be coming to see me, as he had spoken to her earlier in the day while I was meeting with the office manager. Tim said the informant stated she wanted to provide information directly to me while I was out at the division. Tim said he had spoken with outside counsel, and that outside counsel approved of my speaking with the informant based on her request to meet with me. I told Tim I would talk with him later, and ended our call.

CHAPTER 9

TRACKING DOWN LEADS
(THE PLOT THICKENS)

I took out my notebook, recognizing it was getting quite full from all my notes I had been taking. I knew I had another blank notepad in my bag if needed. I introduced myself, and the informant indicated she already knew who I was. I asked her why she wanted to meet. She said she wanted to tell me things about what was happening at the division. I told her that I wouldn't enter her name or refer to her in my notes, but that by meeting with me, she was potentially creating problems in maintaining her anonymity. She said she understood the risks, but thought it would be better to help by providing the information she knew.

She started by telling me the woman in the office I refer to as "the mole" had a close relationship with the controller, having worked together at their previous place of employment. She stated the woman was brought to the division by the controller, and that the woman was not to be trusted. She said that when she spoke with the woman about what was happening at the division, co-worker to co-worker, unbeknownst by the woman that she was speaking with the informant, the woman indicated that she had been in regular contact with the controller and the office manager. She stated the woman said they had told her not to worry, and that they would be back to work soon as there was nothing to be found in a financial review of the division.

She said the woman wasn't paid much and had personal issues, with associated costs exceeding her means. She said that when we ultimately received the monthly United Alliance statements, we would see personal expenses charged to the United Alliance account under the woman's card activity. She said the controller was very much aware of the charges, but allowed the woman to use the card to make ends meet with her issues.

I asked her where the United Alliance statements and information were maintained. She said the controller kept the United Alliance activity in his desk. I thought about the first day and the controller removing papers from his desk with Tim observing his actions. She pretty much confirmed my belief that the controller removed the evidence we were seeking when he left with the papers. I asked her how she came into possession of one of the United Alliance statements, the one she had given to Tim. She said she noticed the statement on the controller's desk, and copied it without him knowing. She said she made a quick copy and put the statement right back on his desk. He was not in the office at the time and did not know the statement was even copied. I asked her if the office manager had knowledge or possession of the United Alliance activity. She said the mail came to the division each day and the office manager opened and reviewed all the statements and invoices. Included were the monthly United Alliance statements. She said she believed the office manager opened and reviewed the activity on the United Alliance account, then provided the monthly statement to the controller.

I asked her if she knew how the United Alliance account was paid. She said she didn't have any idea how the account was paid. I asked her if she was familiar with the bank accounts and bank statements. She said she had no information about the bank accounts, other than seeing the bank statements time and again on the office manager's desk. I asked her if she knew anything about the one identified account. She said she was not familiar with the account.

I then asked her if she knew of any other schemes or issues perpetrated at the division beyond the United Alliance account. She in turn asked me if I had asked anyone about how credit card payments to the organization were handled. I told her I had discussed credit card payments with the office manager and the woman who worked with the office manager (a.k.a. "the crier"), and provided her a brief review of my understanding. As she listened, I watched her shaking her head, anxious to cut me off and interject, but allowing me to finish. As soon as I finished, she said that I described the ideal process of how it was supposed to work. I asked her to describe for me how it actually worked.

She said members would come in to make a payment using their credit card. If the woman was at her desk, the woman handled the payments and processed the charge on the member's card while they waited. However, if the woman was not in or available, the office manager would handle the transaction. The office manager would obtain the card information and may or may not process the charge right away while the member waited. Sometimes the office manager processed the charge, and other times he simply collected the information to process at a later time. He would mark the member's invoice or slip as paid, and tell them their slip would act as a receipt. The payment wasn't processed, the member didn't sign a charge slip, and no receipt was written out from the book. She said many nights, the end-of-the-day close-out of the credit card terminal was never processed, and at times it could go for a week or more before the terminal was closed. She suggested that I look further into the daily close-out and reconciliation of credit card payments by members.

As she described the delay in processing the charges by the office manager, it dawned on me that the office manager could have had different schemes occurring through the credit card payments. One scheme was that the office manager simply didn't charge members' cards. I failed to see how the office manager would have personally benefited from not processing charges to members' cards, and not documenting their payments with receipts from the receipt book. I thought maybe the office manager was simply lazy, or perhaps didn't know how to process charges and didn't want anyone else to know it. These possibilities made no sense to me.

I then thought it could have involved the office manager offering members who came in to pay by credit card a discount if they paid him directly in cash. He could have diverted their payments and made it look like he was taking a credit card payment, knowing that he would never process a charge as the member had already paid by cash (directly to him).

I thought of a third possible scheme where the office manager could have been accumulating unprocessed charges, and on days when he diverted funds through some other means, he could have used the unprocessed charges to fill the void left from his theft.

For now, it didn't matter. The information she was providing only showed me that the office manager had lied to me in the interview regarding how the credit card processing worked. I asked her what else was happening at the division. She said that when I had received and reviewed the United Alliance account activity for the past few years, it would all be there for me to find. I asked her if she thought anyone else was involved with the United Alliance account or any other fraudulent activity at the division. She said she didn't know, but that the three people we had been discussing were definitely involved. She suggested that I speak with each employee of the division. I told her I planned to talk to the remaining individuals including her before I finished the financial review.

Since she came to see me, I had one last question I needed to ask. I knew she might not answer me, but I had to know if there wasn't some hidden agenda or personal vendetta being pursued by the informant by providing information about the controller and assisting with the investigation.

LEARNING POINT

It is not uncommon for whistleblowers or individuals providing you with information to have their own agenda. Anonymous tips could be genuine, or they could be false and misleading, directed toward affecting someone they are targeting or diverting attention away from themselves. A common motive for leaving false tips, especially if hotlines are available, may be revenge, jealousy, personality differences, or other personal issues unrelated to the tip or information provided. Leaving a false accusation is a quick way to put someone you don't like under a microscope, or worse.

It is important to keep an open mind when reviewing tips and information provided, to ensure the information is reliable and worthy of an investigation.

I asked her why she took a chance copying the United Alliance statement and why she came forward with the information. I watched her the entire time I asked the question to see how she would react. Without hesitation or any obvious signs of deception in her body language or demeanor, she said she had thought something was going on financially for quite some time, but was never able to put her finger on it. She said she never had access to the financial aspects of the division, and although she had a hunch that the controller was using the card for personal purposes, it wasn't until she saw the statement left on the desk, likely in error. She said she knew something wasn't right with how the office manager processed credit cards, but thought that maybe the office manager simply left the information for the woman to process when she was available. She said she thought that if she started asking questions to learn more about what they were doing, especially without knowing if others could be involved, it could jeopardize her employment at the division. She also said that she waited until she had positive proof that something was happening.

I suggested to her that she not talk about the matter with anyone, and simply sit back and wait for the investigation to be completed. I cautioned her that if she spoke with too many people or said the wrong thing to the right person, she could end up identifying herself as the source leading to the financial review. She said she planned on keeping quiet and would wait to see what happened. I thanked her for stopping by and talking with me. I reached out and shook her hand as she stood up, then she turned and walked out of the office.

• • •

Back to my notebook to fill in the information she provided. I wondered how I was going to determine what the office manager was doing with the credit card payments. It was going to be like looking for a needle in a haystack. The office manager didn't process charges on a regular basis, but rather merely filled in at times. The office manager didn't fill out receipts, so I wouldn't be able to identify anything from the receipt books. The office manager may or may not have ever processed the charges, so they may or may not have been included within the merchant statement of activity (the monthly credit card details). If the charges were never processed, there would be no way of determining who the members were who paid either by cash to the office manager, or by credit card for those never processed. How was I going to figure this out? Members could pay their dues, as well as pay for program fees and other separate fees such as trips and apparel.

Membership payments could be reconciled, by comparing the membership roster for a period to the payments received by individual members pertaining to the same period. Members who were active on the roster should have corresponding payments in the system. If, however, some payments from members were diverted, and payments from other members were applied to the earlier diverted members' accounts to conceal the diversion (also known as *lapping*), the reconciliation could become very time and labor intensive, if it could be completed at all. With regard to other types of payments, I hadn't thought of a way to reconcile the activity and compare it to something to ensure all the payments had been accounted for.

Part of me knew that I was going to find that the actions of the office manager in processing (or not processing) member credit card payments was linked somehow to the bank account missing all the details that was likely used to pay the monthly United Alliance statements. If I was to find it true that the diverted funds were deposited into the bank account only to be used to pay down the United Alliance account, and that the office manager never used his card for personal purposes as he stated in our meeting, I wondered how the office manager would have personally benefited from doing all this in the first place?

I figured the fastest and most efficient means to determine what went through the bank account, and what comprised the deposit details into that bank account, was to push Tim harder to get the monthly statements and deposit details from the bank.

I made a quick call to Tim to share the new information that the informant provided. I told him he should echo the warning I gave to the informant about keeping quiet or running the risk of divulging her identity as the informant. He said if he spoke with her again in the future he would reinforce what I had told her today. I asked him to get me the bank statements and deposit details from the bank as quickly as possible. I told him I was going to continue reviewing other aspects of the case rather than jump into a very time-consuming reconciliation of credit card payments, to save the organization both time and money, but also that the bank may provide us all the information we need within the statements and deposit details, precluding our having to spend significant time and cost reviewing the credit card activity.

● ● ●

After a brief conversation with the human resource director, I headed back to the boxes. As I drove back, I remembered seeing receipt books in the boxes, not too many of them, but there were some in the boxes. However, I didn't remember seeing much in the way of credit card information. I knew I would have remembered if I saw a monthly merchant statement, but what about the individual charge slips and the terminal close-out slips?

When I arrived I went and found the senior accountant. I discussed the meeting I had with the office manager, and told him I wanted his help looking through the boxes for any credit card activity. Together we went to the storage room where we found the evidence tape intact across the door. As he slit the tape to allow us to enter, I recorded the date and time in my notebook. I then retrieved my notes regarding the contents of each box. The contents were not specific to every item in the box, but rather provided an overall description of what was within each box.

We located two boxes that appeared to contain information we were looking for. One box came from the woman's desk (the crier), and the other originated from the closet where older records were maintained by the division. I locked the storage room, and we each brought a box into the room we had been using all along. We emptied the contents of each box onto a separate table and sorted through the contents. In the first box we found a manual receipt book along with charge slips. There were no close-out or end-of-day slips, and the receipt book appeared to be only the most recent book that was still in use when we arrived on the first day. I flipped through the receipt book and identified two distinct handwriting styles, one much more prominent and frequent than the other. While not a handwriting expert, the more common handwriting appeared to me to be the handwriting of a woman. The other handwriting style on the receipts was much more rushed and mechanical. I surmised the frequent handwriting was that of the woman, and the less frequent handwritten receipts were likely completed by the office manager.

As I flipped through the book I also recognized that the payment methods selected for the more frequent handwriting included cash, check, and charge methods. When I focused only on the second handwriting style receipts, I didn't see any that were marked *paid* by credit card or cash. The only receipts I observed in that handwriting were for payments received by check.

I sorted the charge slips we found, and reviewed each individual slip. There were only a few slips, and nothing unusual was noted on them. I figured the slips and end-of-day close-out reports must have been forwarded by the woman to the office manager for reconciling and recording into QuickBooks each day, and therefore a folder or file must have existed somewhere with all the day's charge slips and close-out reports contained within it. It was not to be found in this box.

We turned our attention to the second box. There were two older receipt books in the box. In flipping through the pages, I noticed the same handwriting styles, with the majority of the receipts completed in a woman's style of handwriting. Just as we had done with the other box, we looked for charge slips, terminal close-out slips, and merchant statements, but none were found.

LEARNING POINT

As a fraud examiner, it is important to obtain a basic understanding of handwriting, and how to identify basic patterns within handwriting. Much information is available to obtain such understanding without having to become an expert in the field. It is also important to identify a handwriting expert who can be brought into a case to expand upon your basic knowledge should the handwriting in question become a key element of the case, such as with forgeries.

The fraud examiner should be able to recognize the significance of handwriting within the context of a case, and preserve any relevant evidence in such a way as to allow the handwriting expert to examine the evidence.

In this case, it appeared to me that a woman likely wrote the majority of the receipts, and that a different handwriting style was used for a lesser portion of the receipts. The second handwriting style appeared to be that of a man's writing.

FRAUD FACTS

Analyzing handwriting is a long, careful process that takes a lot of time and, under ideal circumstances, a lot of comparison samples, or exemplars (documents that have a known author). It's not a matter of looking at two documents and saying, "Hey, they both have a 'B' with a down stroke extending below the line—same author!" In the case of the Lindbergh kidnapping in 1932, the police had a slew of questioned documents. In all, the

(*Continued*)

kidnapper sent 14 notes to Lindbergh with ransom instructions. Handwriting analysts had no problem determining that all of the ransom notes were written by the same person. But preexisting exemplars from the main suspect, Richard Bruno Hauptmann, were scarce, so the police had to get samples from Hauptmann in the police station by way of dictation. From those requested exemplars, handwriting analysts determined a match.[1]

It was starting to look like payments by credit card were not processed, but that would mean the division's revenue should be less than expected based on the number of members and the programs offered beyond membership. I needed to know if all of the members' payments were properly deposited into the division's bank accounts.

I asked the senior accountant to perform a reconciliation of the member payments to the actual bank deposits for a one-year period. I instructed the senior accountant to use the member listing contained within the computer system, and multiply each member by the average membership fee. Once calculated, I instructed the senior accountant to then obtain all the bank statements for the division for the same period and enter all the deposits to the division's account(s) into a spreadsheet. I told the senior accountant that the actual payments (deposits) should come out higher than the calculated fees based on the program fees and other user fees collected from members.

LEARNING POINT

With the potential for theft of receipts, it is important early on in the engagement to determine if the payments documented through whatever system the victim organization used, computerized or manual, reconcile to the actual bank deposits for a given period. For example, the documented payments received for each month should reconcile to the actual bank deposits made for the same month, taking into account any timing differences and deposits in transit. With remote deposit capture (desktop depositing) growing in popularity and use, the timing differences should be lessening. If the payments received (as documented by the organization) do not reconcile to the actual deposits, then the differences need to be

(Continued)

(Continued)

resolved. If the bank deposits are greater than the payments documented, there may be other items included within the deposits that are not payment related. If the payments are greater than deposits, hopefully the organization maintained sufficient details regarding each bank deposit to allow you to research individual deposit items within each deposit, and compare that detail to the individual documented payments for the same time periods. By reconciling deposit by deposit, the differences should be identifiable (provided deposit details are maintained by the organization). Without those details, it may be impossible to determine the differences in detail, such as in the case of a lapping scheme.

I returned to the box listing to see if there were any other boxes that could contain the missing receipt books and credit card slips. I didn't find other possible boxes, but reviewing the list reminded me of the box containing the controller's laptop. We had seized the laptop on the first day and sealed it closed with evidence tape, only to forget about it for a few days. I needed to talk with Tim about what, if anything, could we examine on the laptop retrieved from the controller's office.

I left the senior accountant in the room with the two boxes and headed off to Tim's office. He wasn't at his desk, but I could hear his voice from down the hallway. I followed the sound of his voice until I reached him, and asked him if he would be returning to his office. He said he would be right back. I headed back toward his office, and within moments he was back at his desk.

I asked him if he had discussed the controller's laptop with counsel. He said he had not, and suggested we call counsel together to discuss the laptop issue. We called counsel, and the first question we were posed was if we determined if the laptop belonged to the division or the controller personally. I suggested that since the controller consciously left the laptop on his desk, that it likely belonged to the division. Counsel asked if we had found any evidence of the division buying a laptop in the past year or so. I stated we had not, but we also didn't set out to look specifically for any purchases of laptops. I suggested that I review the QuickBooks activity to see if there were any computer purchases in the past year. If I found any transactions, I would look through the boxes of evidence to see if we had original invoices for the purchase matching the laptop. Based on that discussion we decided it would be best to leave the laptop sealed as is until we better determined whom it belonged to.

LEARNING POINT

While the laptop may not seem significant, determining whether to access the laptop or not could impact the integrity of the entire case. It is not uncommon for a suspect to set up the victim organization, creating a means for a counterclaim against the organization. The controller may have left his personal laptop behind intentionally, expecting us to dive right into his hard drive and access all his personal information. Then, he could claim an invasion of his privacy or some similar claim, potentially diverting some of the attention from the focus of the investigation—his potential thefts from the organization. It would be unfortunate to the investigation and the organization for us to have taken such detailed measures to ensure the admissibility and integrity of all other collected information, only to have the laptop cloud all our efforts. The case was progressing nicely, and the laptop would have to wait until ownership and access issues were resolved.

While we had counsel on the phone I shared a brief summary of my interview of the office manager, as well as my conversation with the informant. Based on my description of information obtained through those meetings, we collectively decided that we would likely find that member payments were being diverted into the identified bank account and used to pay the United Alliance account. Without forming any conclusions or proceeding with tunnel vision, the scheme made sense since all of the items related to that scenario were not found with all the records collected from the division. It had to be more than a mere coincidence that we didn't have the member credit card charge slips, terminal close-out slips, manual payment receipts, bank records for the identified bank account, or the United Alliance statements. I knew, in time, we would have the pieces to put the scheme together. The question that still remained in my mind was whether there were other schemes perpetrated at the division.

I returned to the senior accountant, who had put the records back into the respective boxes and was now working on his laptop with an Excel spreadsheet. I carried the boxes back into the storage room, closed and locked the door, and sealed the door again, noting the time in my notebook. I asked the senior accountant if he needed anything further of me today, and he indicated he was all set and would be working on the analysis for the rest of the day. I decided to end my day and return to my office to attend to other matters.

CHAPTER

10

DRAWING CONCLUSIONS
(WHAT DOES IT ALL SHOW?)

In the morning I went directly to my office to work on another matter with an approaching deadline. I had been out of the office dealing with Tim and the division for several days, and my other client matters were not getting any attention during that time. Plus, without the bank statements and United Alliance account information, I could spend days looking for other clues and schemes, only to drive up the time and cost on the engagement. Instead, I spoke with Tim by cell phone at the end of the day yesterday, and we decided that it would be prudent for me to put a hold on performing any further procedures for a few days to see if the bank information became available.

Later in the day, I called Tim to see if he had heard anything. He said he spoke with the bank, and that the research department of the bank was stretched thin with similar requests. The bank told him that they would need a few more days to get him the requested bank statements and account details. He said he decided not to press them and could live with waiting a few more days for their information. Tim said in the meantime, he would be working with the human resource director to find more permanent solutions for running the division. Tim indicated he had contacted outside resources that could step in and help perform the payment processing, bill payment, and bookkeeping for the division until a permanent solution was identified. Tim said the human resource director would continue to be responsible for processing the division's payroll in the interim.

Planning for business continuity is equally as important as planning for a potential abrupt disruption within the victim organization. I refer to this as the "day-after" plan. The first part is easy—storm the location, remove their computers, secure all their documents and files, and place all the employees on leave. Phase two is much harder but much more detrimental to the future of the organization. Consider things like who will answer the phones, process transactions, make sales, collect payments, complete purchases, process payments, record and transmit payroll, and do all the other tasks of running the organization tomorrow once individuals are placed on leave. Also, how will any transactions be completed without the computers?

Consideration for communications and employee morale must be part of your day-after plan. What message will be communicated to the remaining employees, to customers, to vendors, to the payroll provider, and anyone else? There will be questions, lots of them, and it is best to have contemplated what will happen the day after and implement the plan to minimize interruptions within the organization.

I continued to check in with Tim and the senior accountant pretty much every day. The senior accountant was working on the analyses and calculations, but ended up putting the matter aside to work on other assignments. I needed to get the senior accountant to continue and finish the calculations, or at least send it to me to finish.

Three or four days later, I received a call from Tim. He said he received the bank information for the identified account, and had already made a copy of the information for my use. I told him to have a second copy made for his use, and that he should preserve as evidence the original information provided by the bank. Tim agreed.

Copies and images received from the bank constitute evidence. Although the originals likely reside with the bank providing the records and you are provided copies, it is best to treat the documents received as evidence, properly labeling, preserving, and safeguarding them for future admissibility. Although the bank could possibly provide their original research and

(Continued)

documents at a later date, through the passage of time and changes within a bank's structure, systems, and ownership, the information may not be available at a later date.

Your documentation accompanying the evidence should include when you received the bank-provided information, from whom you were provided the documents, by what method (fax, mail, PDF . . .), the contents and description of the information received, and any other pertinent information. If I receive it by mail, I preserve the original envelope it was received in as well.

I told him I would drive over to collect my copy of the bank information. He told me he noticed that a significant amount of money had moved through the account during the period, and that electronic payments were made monthly from the account to United Alliance. Tim also told me there were checks written from the account, and the checks appeared to be mainly personal in nature. He said the volume of checks and the amounts were minor compared to the payments to United Alliance. Tim indicated that he had already provided the bank information to the senior accountant, who was entering the account activity into a spreadsheet. I asked Tim how far along the senior accountant was with the spreadsheet, and Tim said he would check for me. He put me on hold while he called the senior accountant, and when he returned to our call he said the senior accountant told him he would have it completed by the morning. I thought about driving over, only to have to return tomorrow to get a copy of the spreadsheet. I told Tim I would wait until the morning to retrieve the records and the senior accountant's completed spreadsheet. I told Tim he should put the bank originals in an envelope, mark the envelope as evidence, and maintain the envelope in a secured fashion until tomorrow. Tim said he would ensure that happened as soon as a second copy of the information was made for my use. I ended by asking Tim to tell the senior accountant to e-mail me the spreadsheet if he happened to finish it before the end of the day. My day ended without receiving the spreadsheet, and having no idea what level of activity and transactions they had seen within the bank account.

• • •

The next morning I went straight to Tim's office after completing my morning routine. Tim was in his office, but the senior accountant was not at work as of yet. Tim waved me into his office, and handed me a stack of bank statements and supporting information. He then opened a spreadsheet on his computer and showed me a preliminary summary of the account activity he had received from the senior accountant. He said the senior accountant had not completed his review of the spreadsheet to ensure it was complete and accurate, and that was why he hadn't forwarded it to me. He scrolled down the spreadsheet to the bottom of the columns where the senior accountant had entered formulas to total the activity within each column.

It was early, but my eyes opened wide when I saw that deposits into the account totaled more than $235,000. I asked Tim what period the bank-provided information covered. Tim scrolled to the top of the spreadsheet to find the earliest date, and we both saw that the $235,000 covered a period of nearly five years. I scrolled down the column and noticed the deposits were sporadic rather than at regular intervals. There were also some deposits that were much larger than the typical deposits into the account. I asked Tim if the bank had also provided the deposit details—the copies of the deposit slips along with images of the detail items that comprised each deposit. Tim said they had provided copies of only the monthly statements for the account. I asked him to use the deposit listing and make a request of the bank for all the deposit details for all the deposits into the account. We scrolled through the list and counted more than 200 individual deposits throughout the period. Tim said he would go over to the bank today with the list to request the deposit details.

My focus then moved over to the United Alliance payments made from the account. The electronic payments to the credit card company spanned as far back as the deposits into the account. The total of the payments to United Alliance was around $175,000. The remaining disbursements from the account were in the form of checks, and the check images were not included with the bank-provided statements. Scanning through the list, there were far fewer checks written from the account than deposits. Checks were written on a sporadic basis, and there was no pattern to the timing or amounts of the checks. I told Tim to bring the listing of checks with him and include them with the request to the bank. I knew based on my own experience that even though the organization was a good client to the bank, it would take the bank some time to complete and provide the requested deposit and check details.

The statements indicated the account was closed shortly before our initial visit to the division. One theory I had was that the account was closed, and the new account was opened, simply to shift the activity from the old account into a new account, to limit the chances of discovery of the scheme.

I was really surprised by the volume and amount of deposits and United Alliance payments. I knew there was a likely issue with personal use of the division's credit card based on the credit card statement provided, but I didn't expect in a division of this size to have a theft issue in the hundreds of thousands of dollars. As I thought back to the initial visit to the division, and how the controller reacted and made sure he left with all the evidence, the whole thing was starting to make sense to me. In the papers he took with him were likely the deposit details, bank statements, United Alliance statements, and plenty of other corroborating evidence regarding the scheme.

I thought about the division's financial operations and their annual budget, and wanted to determine what impact the $235,000 would have had on the division's financial picture over the five-year period. Using quick calculations, I broke the $235,000 down into an annual estimated amount of about $47,000. Next I broke the annual amount down into monthly amounts of $3,917, followed by a weekly estimate of about $980. The two largest components of the division's revenues were membership fees approximating $800 per year per member (*fees varied*), and program fees charged to members who signed up for programs not included with their memberships. If the $980 was a fair estimate of weekly diversion of funds, that would mean the fees of one to two members, or $800 to $1,600, would have had to have been diverted almost weekly to reach the annual estimated amount of $47,000 (approximately $980 × 52 weeks). I figured potentially somewhere around 90 or more members would have had to have been left off the membership roster, as well as their membership fees diverted, to have funded the scheme. I thought it was plausible, especially since the division's internal controls tracking members versus nonmembers were grossly inadequate. However, based on a membership population of nearly 900 members, I was finding it hard to believe that roughly 90 members, or 10 percent of the total member population, were not included within the membership database, with their membership fees diverted into this bank account. Plausible—yes; but realistic—no. There had to be other explanations for the sources of funds that comprised the deposits into this account, especially the larger, less frequent deposits I noticed when we scrolled through the spreadsheet. I knew the deposit details and check images would provide us with the information to answer these questions, but I also knew I would have to wait for the bank to produce those details. Waiting for information to continue an investigation can be very frustrating.

I reviewed the list of United Alliance payments made from the account. The payment amounts varied by month, with some months lower than $1,000. All of the other months were significantly more. Some payments, such as those in the summer of 2005, averaged in the tens of thousands of dollars. I knew the only way we were going to determine what the United Alliance account was used for was to get the United Alliance details for the entire period. More waiting for information.

• • •

I asked Tim where we stood with the request to the controller, asking him to turn over the United Alliance statements and information in his possession, or requiring him to request the statements and account details directly from United Alliance to turn over for our review. Tim said he had received his draft back from counsel, and that it could go out to the controller as early as today. I strongly suggested to Tim that he send out the request as quickly as possible. I told Tim the sooner we determined if the controller was going to provide the United Alliance statements and activity, the sooner we would know if Tim would have to initiate a civil case or commence a criminal action in order to gain access to the United Alliance account details. I asked Tim to send me a copy of the request for my files when he sent it out to the controller.

With that I asked Tim if he would have the senior accountant e-mail me his spreadsheet for my files, and also asked Tim to let me know how he made out when he went over to the bank. I figured I wouldn't spend much more time looking at the bank account activity, as the statements had already been summarized in a spreadsheet, and I needed to wait for the deposit and check details to be produced by the bank to go much further. Tim handed me my copies of the bank statements, and said he would retain custody of the bank-provided copies along with all the other evidence. I provided Tim with an envelope and evidence label, and documented the evidence item consistent with all the other items collected and securely stored in the storage room.

I left Tim and drove to my office where I spent the next hour or so documenting in my notes the morning meeting with Tim along with the developments with the bank account. I realized I forgot to check the status of the revenue analysis being prepared by the senior accountant, so I called him. The senior accountant said he had finished the analysis of member revenue compared to actual deposits per the division's operating account bank statements, as well as to the reported member revenue per the division's annual financial statements. He said the amounts within each year were reasonably consistent when compared between calculated member revenue, bank deposits, and reported amounts.

I thought about what he said for a moment, wondering how that could be, knowing the office manager was likely stealing members' cash payments and substituting member credit card payments to conceal the thefts. Then, I figured any members excluded from the division's database (those with their payments diverted) would not have been included in the senior accountant's analysis. Therefore, only the members included in the database multiplied by an average annual rate would have been used to compare to the division's deposits and reported revenue. That analysis would work, as it was all based on the revenue that was actually collected *and* deposited (i.e., the members whose fees were not diverted). While it was important to know if the amounts reasonably reconciled, the analysis wasn't going to provide much more at this time to further the investigation.

It wasn't until the end of the day that I received an e-mail from Tim along with an attached file. The file was a copy of the final letter sent to the controller requesting the United Alliance information. Tim wrote in his e-mail that the letter went out certified mail, and that he expected the letter would reach the controller within a day or two. Tim also said he checked in with the bank, and that they were processing his request for deposit details and check images. Attached to Tim's e-mail were the senior accountant's files that I had requested. Just as with the bank request, we now had to wait until we received a response from the controller. The good news was that it seemed like we were progressing toward resolving the matter.

• • •

I was preoccupied with other client matters for the next week or more, checking in with Tim pretty regularly, but otherwise in a holding pattern waiting on information. It wasn't until the second week that I received a call from Tim. Tim said he had received a large envelope mailed to him, and within the envelope were copies of the monthly United Alliance statements. He asked me if I wanted to get a copy. I told him I would be right over.

By the time I arrived at Tim's office, copies of the statements had already been made for me and for the files. In that limited time, Tim and the senior accountant had scanned the monthly statements, only to confirm what the informant had said all along. The account contained three separate cards issued to named individuals: the controller, the office manager, and the woman (a.k.a. "the mole"). The charges included on the controller's card included lavish meals at restaurants, fuel purchases, food purchases, store purchases personal in nature, online shopping, travel expenses for several trips (especially in the summer of 2005), and other non-business-related expenditures.

There was very minimal activity within the card issued to the office manager. Two charges during the entire period were noted, consistent with what he described during the second interview. The woman's card, however, contained a steady level of charge activity, never for large amounts, but frequent and consistent purchases all appearing to be personal in nature, mainly for pharmacy purchases and other expenses.

The last statement showed the account balance had been paid in full, and that there were no new charges. No subsequent statements were provided. Nothing provided indicated the United Alliance account had been closed out, but rather just that the account balance had been paid. I sat across from Tim at his desk and started thumbing through my copies of the statements. Restaurant meals, groceries, airline tickets, hotel costs, and purchases with vendors who appeared to have no business purpose to the division. Some purchases made within the controller's card activity seemed legitimate business expenses, but not many. The senior accountant offered to enter all the charges for the three cards into a spreadsheet to summarize the activity and allow further analysis. That made sense to me, seeing that he had prepared all the other spreadsheet analyses. I asked him to send me a copy by e-mail as soon as he completed it and reconciled it to the actual statements and balances. He said it would likely take him a day or so, but that he would send it over as soon as it was completed.

I asked Tim if it would be all right with him if I returned to the division to talk with the woman again. I remembered that collectively we decided not to place her on paid administrative leave, and that she should be working at the division. Tim approved my idea, and said the human resource director was out at the division preparing the division's payroll. Tim thought it would be a good idea for me to call the human resource director before heading over, to ensure the woman was at work today and also to let her know in advance that I was coming over and why I was coming.

I used Tim's phone to call the division, and the human resource director answered. I asked if the woman was at work, and she said she was at work. I asked her if the woman would be at the division for the remainder of the day, and she said that the woman typically left for home around 3:30 each day. I explained to the human resource director that copies of the United Alliance statements had been received and reviewed, and that I wanted to speak with the woman about her card's activity. The human resource director asked me to find her when I arrived at the division.

Armed with the copies of the United Alliance statements, I drove over to the division. I knew from scanning the monthly statements that the activity within the woman's card was more than "occasional," the frequency she indicated during her interview. I also knew the activity extended back several years, close to the earliest statement provided, which meant she had been using the card longer than she had admitted (she said one to two years during her interview). The only thing I wished I had prepared before I headed over was a total of the activity for the entire period. I remembered her telling me it couldn't be that much based on her occasional use of the card, but I figured it was much more than she had led me to believe. I knew there was an adding machine in the office I had been using for interviews, and so I figured I would add up all her card activity before I brought her in to talk with her again about the United Alliance card usage.

When I arrived at the division, I found the human resource director working away at the office manager's old desk. The woman who worked at the desk across from where she was working was not around. I asked the human resource director if the woman (a.k.a. "the mole") was in, and she indicated she was down the hall working in her office. I asked about the missing woman who sat across the room, and the human resource manager said she had to leave early to do something with her kids, and that she would be gone for the rest of the day.

After catching up with the human resource director I headed down to the office I had previously used for interviews. I dropped my things on the desk in the office, and turned on the adding machine that was sitting on the desk. I entered the monthly purchases for the woman's card, and once each month was entered, I totaled the tape. The activity spanned nearly the entire period provided, and totaled close to $9,000 in charges.

I left the office and went further down the hall to find the woman. She was sitting at her desk, reading something on her computer screen. She recognized me as I walked into her office, smiled, and said hello. She asked me how I was doing, and said it was good to see me again (all things I am sure she really didn't mean).

I asked her if we could talk for a few minutes, and she said sure. I asked her to follow me back to the private office for a few minutes. She got up from her desk and followed me out of her office. I had arranged the chairs in front of the desk in the office, facing each other. I went in and sat in the chair on the right. She followed me and sat in the other chair. She then asked me what I wanted to talk to her about.

I started by reviewing the previous interview, and highlighting the fact that I told her we would be obtaining the United Alliance account statements as part of the financial analysis. I then told her we had received the statements, and that we had totaled the charges made using her card. I waited for a response, but nothing was provided. I told her that her prescriptions and other expenses paid by the United Alliance card totaled nearly $9,000 and spanned the entire period for which the card statements were provided. I reminded her that she had told me that she used the card only occasionally, that it couldn't be that much, and that it spanned a year or two. Here, too, she had no response. I asked her why the statements showed more activity than she had indicated. I then waited for her to say something, anything. I had done all the talking up to that point, and it was her turn to start explaining these things I was uncovering.

I asked her to explain anything I had asked. Her smile was gone and her overall composure changed from the upbeat person I had met in the other office. She said she must have remembered the details differently from what had actually happened. She asked me how far back charges appeared on the card issued to her. I told her there were charges for personal expenses and pharmacy costs as far back as five years. I reached over on the desk and grabbed my copy of the statements along with the tape I had run on the calculator. Holding them out, I asked her if she wanted to review the activity herself. She said she didn't and that the information I had identified was likely accurate. I asked her why she was less than truthful and forthcoming about the charge volume and duration during the first interview. She said she wasn't lying. She continued that what she had provided me was based on her memory and recollection, and not based on reviewing the actual credit card records back through the period. I asked her if anyone else ever used her card to charge purchases. She said no one ever used her card, and that she kept it in her wallet. I asked her if she still had the card in her wallet. She said she took it out a month or two ago when the office manager told her the account was closed. I asked her how she has been paying for the same pharmacy and personal expenses since the card had been closed. She said she had been using her own funds, but that her funds were getting depleted pretty fast. I asked her what her plans were for the costs once her funds ran out. I asked her if she had the means to repay the funds if required to by her employer, and she said she didn't have any funds. I watched her as her eyes began to well up with tears, her bottom lip quivered, and her face started to turn red. She said she didn't know what she was going to do. I knew I had replaced the tissue packet in my bag, and reached over to grab it. I opened the packet and extended it to her, allowing her to grab one tissue (and not the entire packet, which was how I lost the last one). She wiped her eyes, and I gave her a moment to regain her composure. I put the packet near me on the desk, close enough to me so that I could offer another if needed, and far enough from her so that I wouldn't lose the packet to her.

I reminded her that she had told me the office manager opened and reviewed the monthly credit card statements, and that the controller paid the monthly amounts for the card. I asked her why the office manager and controller would allow her to use the card for personal purchases. She said they both knew about her situation with the pharmacy and personal purchases and her limited means to pay the costs. She said she used the card for occasional charges, and that neither ever told her she couldn't. I reminded her that her actual usage was much more than occasional, very regular and monthly. I asked her if she had any relationship with the office manager. She was clear when she said she had no relationship with the office manager. I then asked her about the controller. Less clear and convincing, she said she had no relationship with the controller beyond her employment. (I knew there was something that had occurred between them of some nature, but she didn't know that I knew that.)

I asked her why the office manager, who had no relationship with her beyond supervisor and employee, would allow her charges to go through month after month without any reimbursement. She said she didn't know. I asked her if she knew why the office manager didn't point out the personal charges to the controller, to have the controller have her stop using the division's card for personal purposes. She said she didn't have any way of knowing if the office manager pointed out the charges to the controller or not. I told her they both obviously knew of her personal charges, especially since the charges were under the card assigned to her. I gave her a moment of silence to think about what I had just said.

After a few moments she asked me why I hadn't asked her if there was any relationship between the office manager and the controller. That caught me off guard and caused me to take a virtual step back for a moment. Thinking to myself, what had she just told me—that the office manager and the controller had a relationship? Trying not to look surprised by this revelation, I asked her why she brought that up in our discussion. She said it was probably the reason why the office manager let her charges continue on the division's card month after month. I asked her to describe their relationship in her terms. She said they were close. I asked her what she meant by them being close. She said they were very close. I asked her to explain to me what that meant, and she said she wasn't going to say anything further.

LEARNING POINT

Expect the unexpected, and never let your guard down. I may have mentioned those key concepts earlier, and frequently. One of my weaknesses, and likely an issue for most accountants who by training focus on finances, money, numbers, and transactions, is not putting enough thought or emphasis on human factors, such as undisclosed relationships beyond the obvious. Through my own experience in being surprised in my cases, I have developed a greater awareness in contemplating potential undisclosed relationships, such as with individuals having affairs and being related to each other.

Early in a new engagement, I ask questions regarding any known or potential relationships, and I enjoy the client's reactions to my questions. In many cases I have to be careful how I ask the questions, and have to explain by providing them examples of my prior investigations of relationships discovered.

FRAUD FACTS

According to all the latest statistics, the workplace has become the #1 place for married people who engage in infidelity to meet the other person.

As women make advances everywhere in society, the old cliché about the boss and the young secretary carrying on an affair has been overshadowed by an increase in the number of men and women who work together as equals becoming romantically involved. The old separation of the sexes has passed and old boundaries to interaction have been replaced by no boundaries. Hearing about the "guys from work" or the "girls at the office" has transformed into the "gang at work."

As we all know, people begin to get to know one another well when working together. The coed workplace offers lots of interaction, teamwork, travel, projects, and longer work hours, all of which lead to members of the opposite sex who share many common attributes growing close. Let's face it, they share the same boss, same work stresses, same lunch hour, and so on.

The unavoidable closeness, commonalities in life, and the amount of time together can lead to friendship. They end up spending a great deal of time, on occasion more time than they spend at home, with this new "friend," so the friendship can become very deep. These friendships can quickly lead to strong emotional attachments. Strong emotional attachments with the opposite sex can often lead to romance. The most noticeable theme is that they work together, grow to understand one another, and "relate" better to this co-worker than they do to their spouse. At home they hear about bills, problems, chores, and so forth. The co-worker friend offers someone who relates to talk with, someone who empathizes with them and does not bring any of the stress that home often has, making them all the more attractive.[1]

I asked her if she had anything else to provide regarding the charges on the United Alliance account. She said that we had covered everything. I asked her if she had anything else she wanted to talk about or add about the division and the finances of the division in general. She said no. I thanked her for her time, and escorted her to the door. As she walked back toward her office, I returned to the desk to update my notebook. I also needed to clear my head for a moment and think about what I had just learned about the office manager and controller.

• • •

As I sat there, unable to write for a few moments, I recalled the interview with the office manager. It was all making sense to me. The office manager may have had his own schemes occurring, but he was also working with the controller in some way, as well as protecting the controller in the investigation. Call me naïve, but up until the past few minutes, when I was struck in the back of my head with a two-by-four, I hadn't considered the possibility of the office manager and controller having a relationship. I thought to myself I would never miss that aspect or consideration in future investigations.

Regaining my focus, I added the notes of our meeting to my notebook, and then went off to find the human resource director. I asked her to join me in the private office for a few minutes, and she followed me back to the office. I closed the door, and walked around the desk. She sat in one of the chairs in front of the desk. I told her I had just finished meeting with the woman, and that she acknowledged charging the $9,000 on the card. I also told her that she stated she is about to run out of personal funds to continue paying the costs, and that she stated she has no means to pay the funds back to the division. I said I think the financial problems of the woman are going to become a real issue in the very near future, if in fact what she said about her inability to pay the costs was in fact true. I said she was going to have to speak with counsel to determine how she was going to address these issues with the woman. The human resource director agreed, and said she would consult counsel to determine how best to handle the woman regarding all the identified issues.

I asked her if she was aware of any relationship between the office manager and the woman. I watched for her reaction while I listened to her response. She said she wasn't aware of any relationship or past issues between the two. I didn't see anything unusual in her body language as she responded. I then asked her if she was aware of any relationship between the office manager and the controller, again watching for her reaction. Her face dropped inconsistently with her prior response. She paused as if trying to think of how to respond to my question. Before she could say anything, I told her that I already knew, and that the woman had just educated me on their relationship. I watched as her head came back up. I asked her how long she knew about it. She said she knew it was likely there was a relationship. I asked her how long she knew, or believed it to be true. She said she knew prior to initiating the engagement involving the division. I asked her if Tim and counsel were also aware of the possibility. She said they were all aware. I asked her why I didn't know this possibility until I stumbled upon it today, weeks after initiating the financial analysis. She said the whole thing was a bit sensitive, and that they felt if there was in fact a relationship, it wouldn't really have any impact on the investigation. She said they had decided to keep that between themselves and counsel as privileged, just in case it turned out not to be true. I sat there dumbfounded, struck a second time, wondering what else they knew but failed to provide to me that could influence the investigation. What she didn't know is that I could have considered other angles within the interview of the office manager had I known the office manager could have been protecting someone else.

CHAPTER 11

CONFRONTING THE SUSPECT
("I DIDN'T DO ANYTHING WRONG")

Not happy about being blindsided with information that was known and should have been provided to me during the planning stages of this investigation, I decided I had had enough of this matter for one day. I ensured my notes were complete and updated, and I left the division. All the way back, all I could wonder about was what else I didn't know that could have an impact or consequence to the whole matter. Albeit the information was sensitive in nature, treated professionally it would have been better to provide it in a controlled fashion with all the appropriate cautions due such information, as opposed to how I actually found it out. I couldn't figure out how they thought it wouldn't come up at some point during the case. I needed to work on something else for a while.

The next day, I received an e-mail from the senior accountant with a spreadsheet file attached. I opened the file and reviewed the United Alliance transactions detailed and summarized by cardholder. As I scanned the activity, I noted there were two charges in the entire period attributable to the office manager's card. Both charges appeared to be business appropriate. I scanned the card activity of the woman, totaling approximately $9,000, and presuming most prescriptions are filled monthly, I identified that there were too many purchases made at pharmacies within each month to be limited to prescriptions only. I figured she had remained less than forthcoming and honest with me, and that many of the purchases at the pharmacies were likely for nonprescription items. I knew she said she didn't retain the charge slips, and that the pharmacies would never provide them upon request due to HIPAA privacy laws and requirements. Either way, all the charge activity of the woman was personal in nature, regardless of her rationalization.

FRAUD FACTS

Your Health Information Is Protected by Federal Law

Most of us believe that our medical and other health information are private and should be protected, and we want to know who has this information. The Privacy Rule, a federal law, gives you rights over your health information and sets rules and limits on who can look at and receive your health information.

What Information Is Protected

- Information your doctors, nurses, and other health care providers put in your medical record.
- Conversations your doctor has about your care or treatment with nurses and others.
- Information about you in your health insurer's computer system.
- Billing information about you at a clinic.
- Most other health information about you held by those who must follow this law.

How This Information Is Protected

- Covered entities must put in place safeguards to protect your health information.
- Covered entities must reasonably limit uses and disclosures to the minimum necessary to accomplish their intended purpose.
- Covered entities must have contracts in place with their contractors and others ensuring that they use and disclose your health information properly and safeguard it appropriately.
- Covered entities must have procedures in place to limit who can view and access your health information as well as implement training programs for employees about how to protect your health information.[1]

In regard to the charge activity of the controller, the senior accountant had established columns to categorize each transaction by type or purpose. Columns included meals, airfare, hotels, purchases, and other, including a column for business-related purchases. I noted there were not many transactions allocated to the last column. It appeared to me that all the activity was personal in nature, and that the reason a separate and undisclosed bank account was likely used to pay the card balance was to conceal this very fact. Still disappointed with yesterday's revelation, I put the information away and returned to working on another matter.

• • •

Within a few days, I received a call from Tim. Tim stated he just received the bank information. I asked him what information the bank provided. He said they produced images of the deposit slips, images of any non-cash deposit items, and images of the checks that cleared the account. I told Tim that I would be over shortly.

It didn't take me long before I was standing in Tim's office doorway waiting for him to wave me in. He pointed to an envelope on his desk, and signaled for me to come in and sit down. I emptied the contents of the envelope onto my side of Tim's desk, and flipped through the pages. Deposit tickets, deposit items, and canceled check images. As I flipped through the stack, I noted that most of the deposit tickets consisted of "cash" deposits, just as we had suspected. The few deposit tickets that contained deposit items other than "cash" were the larger, less frequent deposits. Each deposit, except for one, was supported with an image of the check accompanying the deposit. Each check was written as payable to Crestview and was identified as a donation to Crestview, most of which were paid from estates of prior members and the like for continued support of the organization and their programs. These donations were simply diverted into this private, undisclosed account maintained by the controller and/or the office manager. One deposit contained a notation from the bank indicating the image was no longer available. So I knew we had cash payments diverted along with checks payable to Crestview. With the diverted donations, even fewer members were needed to create the float necessary to fund the unknown bank account.

LEARNING POINT

In conducting a thorough investigation involving the potential theft of funds, it is important not only to quantify the amount of diverted funds, but also to identify and quantify the source of the funds. If, for example, $100,000 of funds were identified as being diverted, then determining where the
(Continued)

(*Continued*)

$100,000 came from to enable the $100,000 to be diverted will help close the loop in the investigation.

In this case, knowing that credit card charges were paid by the organization, it was equally important to determine where the funds came from to fund the payments made on the credit cards. The diverted cash and check payments appeared to be the source of the funds, and the payments to the credit card company appeared to be the use of those funds. As long as the source of the funds approximates the illegitimate use of the funds, the investigation results will make sense and seem reasonable.

The check images were equally interesting. Each check was payable to a vendor for some type of maintenance done at the division. The vendor names were familiar to me, as I had seen many payments to these vendors in the boxes of records. However, for these checks to have been written out of this account, as opposed to the division's primary operating account, there had to be something different about these payments. One vendor in particular was paid for window replacements per the memo notation on each check. I remembered seeing similar payments to the same vendor for window replacement work.

I asked Tim if anyone had copied the bank-provided images, and he said no copies had been made. I volunteered to copy the records, and I made three sets. The first set was for Tim, the second for the senior accountant, and the last for my use. I returned the originals to Tim along with his copy, and suggested that he maintain the bank-provided originals in an envelope marked as evidence similar to the other evidence maintained in the storage room. Tim said he would take care of that. I also handed Tim the senior accountant's copy, as he would likely see him before I did.

I asked Tim if he would have time to review and discuss the bank records, and Tim said his schedule was pretty full with meetings for the day. Seeing no reason to stay, I headed back to my office with my copy of the bank images. Using the senior accountant's spreadsheet of the bank activity, I added a new sheet and began to summarize the deposit information, segregating "cash" deposits from the check deposits. A total of approximately $235,000 in deposits was identified, consistent with the summary of the bank statements prepared earlier. Of the deposits, nearly $35,000 were check payments to Crestview, with the smallest being $500 and the largest nearly $10,000. The donor of the largest payment included the notation "for window replacement" on her check. I figured the check deposited into this account, with checks paid from this account for what appeared to be window replacement work, made sense for now. Of course, I couldn't help but wonder why the deposits and checks weren't processed through the regular operating account, as had been the other payments to the same vendor.

That left approximately $200,000 in "cash" deposits into this bank account. I finished summarizing the deposits and checks, and then I sent Tim an e-mail with a list of the vendors along with the payment amounts. I asked Tim to contact each vendor and have them provide copies of their invoices to support the payments from this account. One vendor in particular, the window replacement vendor, had several payments. I asked Tim to be sure to have each vendor provide the address of where the work was provided for each invoice, to ensure the work was in fact provided to the building at the division and not to the controller's or office manager's personal residence. I was still trying to give both the benefit of the doubt, but I figured the reason these vendors were paid from this account versus the regular operating account was to conceal these payments altogether, as they were funded through cash deposits and diverted checks payable to the organization. Lastly, I asked Tim to have each vendor fax and also mail the copies, mainly so we could get to the information quicker but also have a hard copy for the investigation file.

Tim replied via e-mail pretty quickly, indicating he would have the senior accountant contact each vendor today to obtain the information. Throughout the day, I received copies of e-mails sent out to each vendor by the senior accountant summarizing conversations he had with them requesting their invoices. It was smart thinking, asking for their e-mails to send along a summary, to help ensure they actually sent them over to us.

I started thinking about our next steps in this matter. We had the bank account, the deposits, the checks, and the United Alliance statements and activity. It all seemed to be very straightforward— steal cash payments and checks payable to Crestview to fund an unknown, undisclosed bank account, and use the proceeds to pay for non-business-related personal purchases and activity through an unknown, undisclosed United Alliance account. The vendor payments will likely show the work was not done at the division, but rather at some other location, again for personal gain: $235,000 into the account, and $235,000 out. The one thing we still needed was the controller's explanation for all of these things.

LEARNING POINT

Although it may look like a duck, walk like a duck, talk like a duck, and act like a duck, it still may not be a duck. In order to be thorough and remain objective in an investigation, you need to consider all sources of information even when the findings may be obvious. One source of information would be from the target himself. If you never ask for an explanation of the findings from the target, subsequent information provided by the target explaining the activity may cast doubt over the entire investigation, and put you, the objective investigator, at risk of being labeled biased by not pursuing information from the target. If in the worst-case scenario you issue your report and the target's reputation is negatively impacted publicly, only to learn there was an explanation and you never sought it, you may be defending legal action in the form of defamation, malicious prosecution, or something similar.

I insist that in my engagements we seek out every source of information to explain the activity and findings, even through meetings with the target. If the individual or his counsel refuse to meet to discuss the matter, then you can at least document that you attempted to obtain their side of things.

I ended my day by sending Tim another e-mail asking him if he thought it would be a good idea to have another strategy meeting or conference call to move the case forward. I didn't expect to receive a response so quickly, but Tim responded to my e-mail and indicated we should call counsel in the morning to discuss the next steps. I e-mailed him back suggesting 9:00 A.M., and that I would wait for a call from him or from counsel.

● ● ●

The next morning I retrieved my notes and prepared for the conference call. At precisely 9:00 A.M., Tim called and indicated he had the attorney on the call as well. Tim asked me to summarize what we had revealed to date regarding the account and the credit card activity, and I provided them an overview of the $235,000 activity, along with the nature of the activity. Once I finished, counsel asked what measures were still in process or outstanding. I identified that the senior accountant's requests for the invoices were outstanding, and that once we received the invoices, we would have everything likely to be discovered relative to the accounts and activity. Counsel asked me what I thought the next step should be to bring the investigation to a conclusion. I said I thought a meeting should be set up with the controller, to enable him to be interviewed and to determine if explanations existed for any of the activity and accounts identified. I indicated the controller was on paid administrative leave, and as such, he would be required to come to the meeting to discuss his employment. I said if we didn't provide a means to allow the controller to explain the activity, then if a legitimate explanation existed but was never solicited and the matter moved forward, the ultimate discovery of the legitimate explanation could have a devastating impact on the organization (i.e., the controller could likely sue the organization). By providing a meeting and asking the controller questions, if he chooses not to answer any questions or provide any explanations, then later, even if he provides legitimate explanations, it is clear that he had the opportunity to minimize things but chose not to do so at the meeting (i.e., less luck successfully pursuing the organization).

After a brief discussion regarding the pros and cons of the meeting, who should be present, where it should be held, and what questions should be asked, it was decided that the controller would be requested to come to the main building to meet with me and Tim. It was also decided that Tim would reach out to the controller to set up the meeting and that he would call the controller as soon as our conference call ended. We discussed some potential dates in the next week or so to have the meeting, and we ended the call.

Tim called a very short time later to let me know he had spoken with the controller, who indicated to him that he had counsel representing him. Tim said that the meeting would be held in three days at his building in the conference room at 10:00 A.M., and that because the controller indicated he had an attorney representing him, counsel working with us on this matter would also be present at the meeting. Tim asked me to identify the questions I would like to have asked at the meeting, and to send them along to him and counsel to review in advance of the meeting. We ended our call, and I spent the next hour writing out my questions. I sent them along via e-mail as requested.

• • •

Three days later I arrived at Tim's building early, just after 9:00 A.M. Tim and counsel were getting coffee, and had already put their notebooks and files in the conference room for the meeting. I picked a place to sit across from them, and put my files on the table as well. I met up with Tim and counsel, and we talked about the upcoming meeting. I asked them if they thought he would show up. Counsel thought for sure that the controller would show up, and with counsel. I wagered against counsel, and said I thought he would call, or have his counsel call, just prior to the meeting's start, to indicate there had been a change and that the controller would not be coming to the meeting. I asked counsel and Tim if they wanted to wager against me and my prediction. Neither dismissed my prediction, but neither wagered. I said the options were that he would not show up, he would show up, he would show up with counsel, or he would show up with someone else (for moral support). I again asked if either wanted to wager based on which option they thought was going to happen. Still, no takers.

We sat at the table and spent the next hour going through what we knew to date. At precisely 10:00 A.M., the receptionist indicated that the controller was in the lobby, with his attorney. He showed— counsel was right. Too bad counsel didn't wager—it could have been $3 or $4 if we each bet my standard $1 wager.

We put our serious faces on, while Tim went to retrieve the controller and his attorney. As they entered the room, I realized it was the first time I had really seen the controller, except for the brief glimpses of him on that initial day at the division. His attorney was a well-known criminal defense attorney, someone I had heard much about, but we had never crossed paths. We went around the table exchanging business cards. The controller's attorney began the meeting by preaching about how wrong it was for the organization to come out to the division in the manner that it was conducted, only to ruin the controller's livelihood and his reputation permanently. He continued making his statement, obviously uninformed about what really had happened and the information we had subsequently uncovered justifying the investigative measures taken. Once he finished, Tim indicated that the investigation was not finalized and was still in process, and that the purpose of today's meeting was to solicit information from the controller to provide explanations for the activity discovered. With that, the controller's attorney countered Tim's remarks by stating that he and his client were glad to see the investigation was still ongoing and that no conclusions had been reached in the matter regarding the activity. He continued, stating that he and his client were not prepared today to answer any questions or provide any information.

We all looked at him as if to ask what was the purpose of today's meeting if no information or explanations were going to be provided. Tim stated what we were all thinking and asked the controller's attorney why we set up the meeting if the controller was not going to answer any questions. The attorney responded that the controller was willing to help clear things up, and that if we were to write out all the questions we would likely ask the controller and send the questions to him, he would then provide them to the controller to obtain the answers. A fishing expedition—they were here to find out what we knew to date and also to find out what they could learn about the case against the client, the controller. With that, counsel thanked them for coming in and Tim walked the controller and his attorney out of the meeting and out of the building.

Tim returned a few moments later and we discussed the meeting. Counsel asked me to review the questions that I had previously provided, and asked me to add any further questions. Counsel asked that I review my questions one last time, as should Tim with his own questions, and said that once received, the questions would be compiled into a letter to the controller's attorney soliciting responses.

Counsel then suggested that the investigation move forward without their responses, as no responses would likely be provided. Counsel said the questions would be forwarded as indicated to the controller's attorney during the meeting to show good faith on our part, but that there was no way a criminal defense attorney would allow his client to provide evidence that would only incriminate him. Counsel asked Tim what the organization intended to do with the information known to date regarding each individual.

Tim said there had been discussions within management, and that the controller and office manager should be pursued criminally, as well as civilly, for their involvement in the schemes. I asked Tim about the woman who had the United Alliance card. Tim said we would wait to decide what to do with her, but for now we should start the process with the other two individuals. We discussed the controller's role and how to proceed with his involvement. It seemed pretty clear the controller had been using the organization's funds through his personal use of the United Alliance card, and funding the activity with diverted cash payments and checks. Counsel felt the case against the controller was strong, and that it should proceed as the organization desired. Then, we discussed the office manager's role in the activity. We all agreed that the office manager had knowledge and facilitated the controller's scheme. The question that remained was whether the office manager benefited in any way from the activity by aiding and abetting the controller and by conspiring to commit larceny for the controller's benefit. I was confident that the office manager had benefited from this scheme, as well as through other schemes he likely had that we had not uncovered. The question was whether the information we did have to date was enough to have him charged criminally. Counsel suggested that Tim set up a meeting with the appropriate law enforcement agency to initiate a criminal complaint, and let them help determine the roles and crimes of each individual. I asked if I could be part of that meeting, and they agreed I should be at the meeting.

LEARNING POINT

In many jurisdictions, police involvement begins with an initial complaint being made, often at the patrol officer level. This may differ depending on your jurisdiction as well as each agency's approach to these types of crimes. At the initial meeting, my approach is to provide the minimum level of information required of the agency to initiate a case.

Generally, once the case is initiated or opened, it is often forwarded to a detective or someone more appropriate for these matters. Once assigned and contact has been established, a meeting is set up to discuss the case, as well as provide much more detailed information. Included in the discussions should be the victim's desired outcome of police involvement.

In certain instances, police involvement was not initially wanted by the victim, but during the course of the investigation the target refused to cooperate, leaving few options to getting the matter resolved. If the sole goal of getting the police involved is to get the target's attention to come to

(Continued)

terms with what he or she did and to discuss how his or her actions will be resolved, that too should be discussed up front with the police agency. Some agencies and officers will be willing to initiate a case to get things moving along, knowing the criminal case will likely be discontinued if the target comes to terms in dealing with his or her actions. Other agencies and officers will not want to become involved and expend resources unless arrest and prosecution are the goals. In my experience, law enforcement agencies have limited resources and don't want to invest time and energy acting as pawns to accomplish the victim's goals and objectives outside of an arrest.

DOCUMENTING THE INVESTIGATION
(YOUR WRITTEN REPORT)

Now I had work to do on this matter. Before we could go to the police, we needed to document the case in a fashion that the police could follow, supported by the evidence we collected to date. I knew based on my experience that we would receive the best reception from law enforcement if I created a written report referencing all the procedures that had been performed along with exhibits containing copies of the supporting evidence. Presented with a report or binder, the assigned person would then be able to build his criminal case off the work we had already performed, as well as rely on an independent, objective expert (myself) working on behalf of the victim.

Knowing we were still waiting for the vendors to provide copies of their invoices for the payments that were paid through the undisclosed account, I asked Tim if he wanted me to start documenting my report in the hope that the vendor invoices would arrive before long. Tim said he thought that was a good approach to take, and asked me to let him know when I would be prepared to meet with him and the local police department. I asked Tim to tell the senior accountant to contact me as soon as any of the vendors provided their invoices. I also asked Tim to review the organization's insurance coverage again, to ensure the potential claim was not dependent on meeting certain requirements, such as having the suspect arrested, to get the claim paid. With that I left for my office.

Driving to my office I reviewed different approaches I could use to document my report. I knew my report would have to be identified as "preliminary report" or "initial findings" until the vendor invoices were received. Once the last pieces of information arrived from the vendors I would be able to finalize my report. I reviewed my report's audience as well. In this case I knew my report would be used by counsel in a civil matter, should the organization choose to sue the controller and possibly other involved individuals to recover its funds. I knew my report would be used by law enforcement, a prosecutor, a judge, and/or a jury in the criminal matter soon to be initiated. I also knew my report would likely be used by Tim to support an employee-dishonesty claim with the organization's insurance carrier. Although this range of audiences relying upon my report was typical, I deliberated how best to approach documenting this case.

I spent the rest of the day organizing my thoughts and notes, and spreading out the copies of the evidence collected. I printed the various spreadsheets I had prepared or had received and revised from the senior accountant, and determined which items would need to be added as exhibits to my report to support my findings. Then I started writing.

LEARNING POINT

Writing, reading, editing, and rewriting the report is a very time-consuming period in every engagement. I know when I write my reports, I want to be sure to include all the pertinent details and findings, but at the same time I want the report to be easily read and followed by someone with much less financial experience. As I started to write my narratives, I created references to numbered exhibits that I knew I would need to include to illustrate detailed information and findings.

The approach I use in documenting my report allows my report to stand on its own, meaning that everything needed to support my procedures and findings is contained within my report as an exhibit. In most cases, my report and exhibits need to be presented within three-ring binders. The goal of this approach is that anyone who reads my report can easily go to the detailed exhibits to review the supporting information as well, minimizing the need to ask me for additional information or details. If something were to happen to me once a report was issued, everything needed to substantiate the report contents would still be available directly within my report as attached exhibits.

I continued writing the next day as well. By that afternoon I had drafted my preliminary report based on the procedures performed to date, and had included all the exhibits needed to support my preliminary findings. The next morning I printed the report and sat in my conference room where I read the entire report without any interruptions. I marked up the report with a red marker as I customarily do, and went back to my desk to make all the changes to the actual report file. I saved the updated report with changes to the same file name as the initial report file.

LEARNING POINT

Saving drafts: My experience has shown me that drafts or versions of reports can be problematic to the case if they are retained. While drafts are common as your report is being drafted and ultimately finalized, each draft identifies the changes made since the last draft or version.

A common practice is to never retain drafts, as drafts do not exist. Each time a report is revised toward issuance, the file is saved over the prior file, leaving the sole file on the hard drive. All pages printed for review and revision are shredded and not saved, if printed at all. Drafts are not shared with outside parties, and if a draft is prepared and discussed with an outside party, such as with counsel, then and only then is a hard copy of the draft retained for the engagement files. The electronic file is still overwritten as the report is finalized.

It is important to remain consistent and compliant with your firm's draft policies. In many cases, I find myself reminding counsel who retained me that if I were to produce a draft of my report for their review, then I would have to retain the draft as part of my files subject to discovery by opposing counsel. In most cases, a draft is no longer desired.

Once satisfied with my "preliminary report," I printed a copy and prepared a fax cover letter to counsel. Since we were waiting for vendor invoices anyway, I figured I would have counsel review and approve the report up to this point, and simply update my report once the vendor information was received. I also knew with Tim there would be no way I could finish and issue my report without his prior review and approval of a draft. In my fax cover I asked counsel if I should fax a copy to Tim for his review at the same time. I faxed my report to counsel, and put Tim's copy aside pending approval from counsel.

Later in the day I received approval via e-mail from counsel to send my draft preliminary report to Tim for his review. I faxed it over, and asked him in my fax cover to check with the senior accountant regarding following up with the vendors for copies of their invoices.

FRAUD FACTS

Although the following references to North Carolina and laws vary from state to state, this ruling is the general standard in federal and most state court systems.

"Plaintiff's assertion of the attorney-client privilege to shield discovery of any communications with counsel involving his expert opinions is misplaced. Expert witnesses are subject to specific rules of discovery under the North Carolina Rules of Civil Procedure. Generally, the facts known to and the opinions held by an expert are discoverable as well as the materials the expert relied upon in coming to his or her opinion. If [the expert's] opinions are based upon any information supplied to him by counsel, that information is discoverable and Plaintiff is required to make disclosures of that information."[1]

The drafts, e-mails, approvals, and such in this case all constitute discoverable communications, which is why you want to minimize all communications including what you document in your notes and in your files regarding the engagement.

● ● ●

At the end of the day I called Tim to ask him how he made out reviewing my preliminary report. Tim said he had reviewed the report, and was sending back "suggestions" to clarify things or add more details. Tim knew it was my report and I didn't need to make any changes to address a client's suggestions, but typically the changes suggested are minor and don't change the context or facts in any way. Further, the client typically wants to feel they contributed to the overall investigation, and by suggesting changes to the written report, they have made an impact, albeit a minor one, to my report. I also knew in the end that I, the expert, objective, unbiased, independent forensic accountant, am responsible for the report I issued, and that it must reflect my procedures, findings, and conclusions unfettered by the client or anyone else.

I received and reviewed the suggestions identified by Tim—all minor changes, mainly cosmetic in nature. Nothing was recommended changing or influencing the nature of my procedures, the results, or my findings. I made the changes and saved the file over the original file, leaving only the latest file on my computer drive. Then I called Tim to discuss setting up the meeting with the police. I reached Tim in his office, and indicated that we should start the process using my preliminary report. Tim agreed, and asked if we should provide a quick update to counsel before proceeding. I agreed, and Tim was able to connect with counsel to join us on our phone conversation.

After a brief discussion regarding my preliminary report, counsel said we should proceed. Tim said he would contact the local department to initiate a case. I told Tim that the typical response was for a patrol officer to meet with Tim to take an initial complaint, and once filed, the department would assign someone inside, a detective or someone similar, to handle the case from that point forward. I told Tim that he should provide minimal information to the patrol officer, enough to document a complaint worthy of follow-up by the department, and not provide a copy of my preliminary report. I said once the next person was assigned and contacted Tim, we should meet and review a copy of my preliminary report at that time. Tim agreed with my approach and said he would call today to start the process. I told Tim I didn't need to be at the initial reporting, but that once he was contacted by the individual assigned the case, I wanted to be at that meeting. Tim agreed.

A few hours later I received a call from Tim. He said he met with a patrolman who came to his building and took the initial complaint. Tim said the police officer indicated he would submit his report at the end of his shift, and that the case would then be turned over to the detective division for follow-up. Tim said the officer told him he would be contacted by a detective within a few days. I asked Tim if the senior accountant had received any of the vendor information. Tim said he would check and get back to me. I asked Tim if we could proceed with the insurance claim filing, or if he wanted to wait until the vendor information was received. Tim said he would make that determination once he spoke with the senior accountant.

I received an e-mail from the senior accountant with images of vendor invoices attached. The invoices were from the window replacement vendor. In the e-mail the senior accountant stated each vendor was contacted again today to provide their invoices, and as any were received they would be forwarded to me for review.

I reviewed the scanned invoices and recognized instantly that the work performed was not at the address of the division, but rather at the personal residence of the controller. I updated my spreadsheet of the bank account activity, and allocated the invoice amounts to the controller's column of diverted funds.

By the end of the day two additional similar e-mails were received from the senior accountant. In both cases the invoices reflected repairs or maintenance-type work performed, but the address of service was not identified on the invoices. I called Tim and asked him how we should treat the remaining disbursements from the bank account. Tim said we should check with counsel but prepare to move forward as if no additional invoices were received from the vendors. Tim suggested all the checks be included in the claim, unless counsel felt differently, and let the controller identify and support why each payment should not be included. I agreed with Tim's treatment, but said I would discuss it with counsel before finalizing my report. I called and spoke with counsel, and we decided to adopt Tim's approach for the unsupported payments, allowing me to finalize my report and move the matter along.

● ● ●

The next morning I updated my report, exhibits, and analyses for the vendor invoices that were received, as well as the treatment of the remaining unsupported payments. I read my report one last time, recalculated all the amounts and totals within each analysis or exhibit, and saved the report file over the prior file, leaving only one file on my computer drive (no drafts). I generated final pages of my report along with copies of all the analyses and exhibits. I bound and signed each copy of my report, and reviewed each report one last time for assembly accuracy. I marked each report in a manner consistently used to ensure the authenticity of each report, and prepared the reports for delivery to Tim.

LEARNING POINT

Simple steps can help ensure the integrity of your report is consistent with the integrity of your investigation. Once your report has been finalized, assembled, bound, and signed for delivery to your client, who is likely counsel, a quick flipping of pages within each copy of your report can identify issues in assembly that could undermine your credibility and hard work on the engagement. Obvious things can be easily corrected if identified prior to delivery of your report, things like pages bound upside down or out of order, duplicate or missing pages, and exhibits out of sequence. A rule of thumb at our firm is to sit and flip through each and every copy of every report prior to delivery, page by page, to ensure none of these things or anything else has occurred that could prove embarrassing at the least, damaging at the worst, to our reputation and our standing as an expert in our field.

Even worse could be opposing counsel using one of these easily detected issues within your report against you. If the defense's position contends the activity was a series of undetected mistakes, opposing counsel could use you and your report to illustrate how mistakes could go undetected, and now you and your report could be being used to support the suspect's position.

I drove to Tim's office with the reports, hoping he would be there to provide me with an update regarding the police report. Luck was on my side, and he was in his office. I provided him with the report copies, and asked him if he had heard anything from the police. He said he had received a voice message from a detective late in the afternoon yesterday, but due to his schedule with meetings and other obligations, he had not returned the call. I asked Tim if he wanted to reach the detective while I was in his office, to ensure a meeting would accommodate both our schedules. Tim provided me with the detective's name, and dialed the number left on his voice mail.

The detective was in, and we set a meeting for later in the day. Tim and I would go over to the police station to discuss the case, and bring a copy of my report. While I was in Tim's office I asked him about the insurance claim. Tim indicated he had already completed the claim affidavit, and planned to simply attach a copy of my report to the claim. Tim said he was going to have counsel review the claim affidavit prior to filing, with the goal of having the claim filed within a day or so. I asked Tim to send me a copy of the final claim affidavit filed for my files, and Tim said he would send me a copy of what was filed.

Tim and I drove over to the police station together, bringing a copy of my report. I had my audit bag with my notebooks and other information collected during the procedures, and I knew the originals for the case were still secured in the storage room within Tim's building. I hadn't recently checked the evidence tape to ensure no one had accessed the room, but I was fairly confident the tape would still be intact as it had been every time I did access the room. A middle-aged detective emerged from a closed door on the side of the lobby, and he introduced himself to Tim and me. The detective escorted us back through the door he emerged from and down the hall to a small interview room. We sat at a table, and the detective read the initial report documented by the patrol officer. Once finished, he asked Tim to explain what happened.

Tim ran through a high-level summary of the events from the initial tip through my final report while the detective took notes in his notebook.

13

WORKING TOWARD A RESOLUTION
("I DON'T WANT TO GO TO PRISON")

Tim finished describing to the detective the bank account and credit card activity and our findings. The detective seemed to follow along with the information that Tim was providing, taking notes throughout Tim's explanation. Then the detective looked down at the copy of my report. I told the detective that the case from start to finish was described within my report, along with schedules identifying the activity and copies of the bank and credit card statements. The detective said he wanted to discuss each individual who worked at the division, one at a time, starting with the controller. The detective asked Tim the name and other demographic information about the controller. He provided the information while the detective wrote it in his notebook. The detective then asked a lot of questions about the controller, his role and responsibilities at the division, and the activity on the credit card, as well as the bank account. When the detective asked how much was involved and for what period of time, I opened my report to the schedule that summarized the activity. The detective looked at my schedule, then said that we were dealing with first-degree larceny, a Class B felony in Connecticut, as the amount was in excess of $10,000. In fact, the alleged amount far exceeded the $10,000 threshold, the highest threshold for larceny in Connecticut.

After much discussion about the controller, the detective stated he had a good understanding of the controller's role in this scheme. The detective said he was thinking along the lines of conducting his criminal investigation with a goal of applying for an arrest warrant for larceny against the controller. The detective said he thought it would be very straightforward, and that based on his experience it would be unlikely that the controller would meet with him or provide him with a statement, especially since he had already appeared at one meeting with his defense attorney. We shared with him our experience meeting with the controller and his attorney, where nothing was accomplished. Tim indicated we were still waiting for the information they said they would provide. Neither Tim nor I expected to ever receive anything from them.

Next, the detective asked about the office manager. Tim provided the office manager's name and other demographic information. The detective asked Tim how the office manager fit into the scheme. Tim said that the account statements, credit card statements, and all other financial transactions were received, reviewed, and processed by the office manager, and that even if he didn't personally benefit from the controller's scheme, something neither Tim nor I believed, we did believe that the office manager had knowledge of what had transpired. In essence, the office manager had allowed the controller to carry out the scheme at the division without alerting anyone, a clear breach of his fiduciary duty to the organization. Tim said we both believed the office manager had his own schemes and was likely compensated or benefited in some way by the controller's actions, but that to date we had been unable to identify any other schemes or otherwise show how the office manager directly benefited. Tim stopped short of disclosing the alleged "relationship" between the controller and office manager, something I never acknowledged to Tim that I had learned, and had discussed only with the human resource director. I figured if no one bothered to share that potentially important information with me at the onset of the investigation, then I would keep that knowledge to myself. Also, I figured the human resource director had told Tim that I knew of the relationship based on my interviews. Tim never mentioned the relationship or my knowledge of it during any of our subsequent interactions.

As we discussed the office manager, the detective was as convinced as we were that the office manager was somehow involved in the controller's scheme beyond just allowing it to occur. At a minimum, the detective said he would consider pursuing a conspiracy to commit larceny charge (aiding and abetting, if you will) against the office manager. The detective said the controller would likely implicate others who were involved once he knew he was getting arrested, which was something Tim and I had discussed in an earlier meeting.

Next, the detective asked Tim about the woman who worked in the office. Tim provided her name and information, and stated that although she was an emotional train wreck, nothing had been found to date to show she had knowledge or was involved in any way with the actions of the controller. The detective continued writing notes in his notebook. The detective asked Tim what he wanted to have happen with the woman. Tim said he believed she wasn't involved, and therefore was off our radar screen as far as being prosecuted for anything. The detective said that made his job a bit easier—fewer individuals on whom to focus his efforts.

The detective asked Tim about the woman who maintained a credit card. As with all the others, Tim provided her name and other pertinent information. Tim said that the woman admitted to using the division's card for personal purchases, but that she did so with the full knowledge and approval of the controller. The detective asked Tim for the woman's story. Tim said the woman was not credible, but that her consistent story was that she used the card to pay for personal expenses and prescriptions. I showed the detective the analysis in my report, and showed him how the frequency of drugstore purchases was inconsistent with how most prescriptions are refilled (monthly, bi-weekly . . .). The detective asked Tim if he wanted to pursue criminal charges against the woman as well. Tim said it would likely be a difficult case to prove intent on her part if she acted with permission from the controller, the individual responsible for running the division and making the financial decisions, such as allowing the use of the card for personal purposes. Tim said that she would be pursued civilly for restitution of the funds that she was not entitled to, but that having her arrested was not a goal of the organization.

The detective asked if there was anyone else at the division that he should be aware of, either as a suspect or as a witness to the case. Tim and I had discussed the informant's confidentiality prior to the meeting, and it was decided at that meeting that the informant would not be disclosed when meeting with the police. The police needed to be provided with the facts as we knew them to allow them to initiate a criminal investigation. How the information first came to light was not necessarily germane to their case.

How information was first received in the matter needs to be considered, and specific laws exist protecting whistleblowers. Even if an individual providing the initial information or tip was not promised confidentiality and anonymity, care and consideration should be exercised with regard to the individual and disclosure of his or her identity. Legal counsel should be helping to decide whether an individual's identity and the information he or she provided is ever disclosed.

If the case can be made on the evidence obtained without ever disclosing how the case came to light in the first place, that may be the best avenue to pursue, as we did in this case. In many of my cases the target never knew (or asked) how the case came to light.

Tim told the detective that there were others who worked at the division, but that no one else was identified as potentially being involved in the scheme. The detective asked Tim to name who they were for his notes. Tim provided him with their names and then asked the detective what would happen in the case.

The detective said he would be pursuing the criminal matter, and that he needed to conduct his investigation, focusing on specific violations of the law. The detective indicated that he would be contacting the controller, the office manager, and the woman from the office, to see if each individual would be willing to meet and provide a statement. The detective asked if he could keep a copy of my report, and Tim provided him with a copy for his file. The detective also said he would be applying for search warrants to the controller's and office manager's personal bank accounts, and if received, would share the records with us.

The detective asked where all the original information and the evidence was being maintained. Tim indicated that all the evidence had been properly collected, marked, and preserved to establish a chain of custody, and that all the evidence continued to remain secured in a restricted storage room at his building. Tim asked if the evidence needed to be turned over for prosecution purposes. The detective said that as long as the evidence was being maintained in such fashion as to ensure a proper chain of custody, he didn't need to take the originals today. He said he would discuss the case with his supervisors and the prosecutor, and based on what they wanted to see happen, he would be back in touch with Tim. He said if it was needed initially, he would collect it. Otherwise, he would work from the copies in my report and collect the original evidence later, if needed at all.

With that, the detective wrapped up our meeting, and walked us out to the lobby of the police station. We thanked him for his time, and left.

• • •

Back at Tim's office the insurance claim was returned from counsel with their input. For my review, Tim copied the claim, which we further discussed. Tim said he would copy the claim and supporting information, with the goal of filing the claim by the end of the day. The employee-dishonesty policy had a claim limit of $50,000 with a $1,000 deductible. The organization wouldn't receive all its funds, but it was still $49,000 more than they would likely receive back from the controller. I asked Tim to send me a copy of the final claim he filed for my records, and with that I left Tim and returned to my office.

Back at my office I decided to organize my files for the case. I knew I would be waiting for the three parallel tracks to proceed, being the civil case, the criminal case, and the insurance claim. I also knew the insurance claim would likely be the first to get resolved, followed by the criminal and civil, in that order. It is also not uncommon for the criminal and civil cases to get resolved simultaneously.

LEARNING POINT

There are at least two factions regarding how to proceed in pursuing restitution and resolution in these types of matters. The first faction pursues one avenue, such as a criminal case, at a time, with the hope that the results of the first means (e.g., a criminal case) will have a positive effect on the others (e.g., a civil matter). Therefore, they typically wait on the civil matter until the criminal matter is resolved.

The second faction pursues all options simultaneously, which was what happened in this case. A civil case was initiated at the same time a criminal case was launched and the insurance claim was filed. All three channels proceed concurrently, and the fact that criminal and/or civil cases have been initiated may actually help in getting the insurance claim paid. In some policies, a criminal case is required to get the claim paid.

(Continued)

(Continued)

My attitude is—why wait on any means of pursuing restitution and justice, if those are goals of the victim? Locate and lock down any assets of the target you can before they are gone, as they may be the only means of collecting from the individual. Also, it is not uncommon for the civil and criminal matters to be resolved through one global settlement or agreement.

Two weeks went by before I heard anything further on the case. I received a voice message from the detective asking me to call him. In his message, he stated that he wanted to go through a few things in my report for clarification purposes. I called and left him a voice message, starting the latest round of phone tag. I knew it was common for detectives to have variable work schedules, and given other crimes that were committed in their area, that days or weeks could go by before we ultimately connected. This round of phone tag ended just two days later when I heard back from the detective. It was close to the end of the day, and I was in my office when he called. He said he was working evenings, and had just started his shift (conveniently at the end of mine). He asked if I had time to review my report, as he wanted to clarify a few things that I had written. I told him I had time, and asked him to wait as I retrieved my copy of the report.

With my report now in front of me, I asked him what questions he had with my report. He referred to the exhibits and had me walk him through the information, asking questions about each exhibit. He indicated that he was in the process of writing the search warrant requests, and wanted to be sure he documented his understanding consistently with my understanding of the facts. He said the prosecutor had asked him to keep the requests as simple as possible, using plain English easily understood by any reader, and to keep it as brief as possible.

I asked the detective where things stood with his investigation. He said that he had contacted the controller's attorney, and that they had no interest in meeting except to learn what evidence the police had against the controller. The detective told them it was a meeting for the controller to tell his side of things and the controller's attorney said the controller would not be making a statement. The detective said he was simply moving forward with a search warrant for the controller's bank account and an arrest warrant for larceny charges. The detective said he was applying for them simultaneously, and if evidence came out of the information in his bank accounts based on the search warrant indicating the controller had committed other crimes, that he would apply for a second arrest warrant and arrest him for that as well. The detective said in the meantime there was no reason to delay the controller's arrest for the known items, and get things started.

I asked the detective where things stood with the office manager. The detective said he discussed the office manager and his role in the scheme with his supervisors and the prosecutor, and neither had much of an interest in pursuing the office manager without clear and convincing evidence that he benefited from any crimes. He said the consensus was for the organization to pursue the office manager civilly for breach of fiduciary duty, but that insufficient evidence existed to present a clear and convincing case beyond a reasonable doubt that the office manager had participated in the thefts by the controller. Disappointed but understanding, as that determination was not uncommon, I asked the detective if he would at least interview the office manager to see what information he could provide, as well as put additional stress onto the office manager. The detective said he had already left messages for the office manager to call and set up a time to come in and discuss the matter, but that the office manager had yet to return any of the messages.

LEARNING POINT

Unfortunately, if law enforcement and the prosecutor's office decline a case, that may be the end of the road for the victim. This is especially true if the insurance coverage has been exceeded, and the targeted individual holds no assets or means for restitution. Pursuing the target through a civil lawsuit will cause the victim organization to incur costs in professional fees, and even if a judgment is received favorable to the victim organization, the chances of collecting from the individual on the judgment are poor at best.

Once a criminal case is off the table, and the diverted funds and costs from the insurance and/or the individual are not available for recovery, or the individual is not likely to yield any restitution, there may be no other means of recovery. The victim organization may have

(Continued)

(*Continued*)

no other means and will have to realistically decide to let the matter end. However, the victim organization should consider one last issue—tax treatment of its lost funds, and reporting the diverted funds to the tax authorities. Consideration of both of these issues should be addressed with proper tax professionals, but it is common for the victim organization to take the loss, as it has exhausted all means of recovery of the stolen funds, and issue the individual a Form 1099 for each year funds were stolen from the organization. Once again, I strongly recommend a victim organization talk with their tax professional and attorney prior to adopting either tax reporting strategy.

FRAUD FACTS

In the crime of embezzlement, there are tax implications for both the embezzler and the embezzled. Embezzled income is taxable to the person who does the embezzling.[1] The embezzled amount should be included in the embezzler's gross income in each year of the embezzlement. In addition, the embezzler/employee may be subject to self-employment taxes on the embezzled amount. Since the embezzlement constitutes income to the embezzler, the entity that has suffered the loss *should* report it to the IRS.

Restoration of embezzled funds does not affect the reporting requirement. Income is recognized at the time the embezzler takes control of the funds,[2] and, is, therefore, not affected by subsequent restitution. Thus the embezzler would be required to report the restitution as a miscellaneous itemized deduction subject to the 2 percent adjusted gross income exclusion in the year of the restitution.[3]

I asked the detective when he thought the arrest warrant would be completed and signed, and when he would be arresting the controller. He said that he planned on completing the arrest warrant within the next week or so, and that once it was signed, he would contact the controller's attorney to execute the warrant. I asked the detective to let me know when that happened, and he said he would as long as I kept it between us. I agreed, and asked him if he had any further questions with my report. He said he had what he needed, and thanked me for my help with the case. I wished him luck in completing the warrants.

I called Tim and provided him with an update. Disappointed as I was, Tim thought the office manager should be arrested along with the controller. I suggested we have a conference call with counsel, and bring them up to speed on where things were as far as the criminal aspect. Tim agreed, and he was successful in getting counsel onto our call. I provided a similar summary to counsel as I had done for Tim, and indicated that a decision needed to be made regarding the office manager. I suggested that we end the employment of the office manager, and decide either to pursue the office manager civilly for damages due to his breach of fiduciary duty to the organization, or to simply "close the barn door" with him and move forward. We discussed the pros and cons of both avenues, and given the fact that he lived at home, drove around in his parents' cars, and appeared to have little or nothing as far as recoverable assets that we could attach, we decided to simply terminate him and move on. We all knew that he very likely had schemes occurring and stole from the organization, but the deciding factor was whether it made sense to continue paying professionals' hourly rates to successfully obtain a judgment against the office manager, only to have no means of collecting on the judgment. We all knew it was the right decision for the organization based on the known facts, but letting the office manager off the hook and allowing him to walk away from all this just didn't seem right. Tim said he would speak with the human resource director, and share with her our decision to terminate him, and that he should be terminated as of today. With that we closed the book on the office manager.

• • •

While I had Tim and counsel on the phone, I asked about the status of the woman who had used the credit card for personal purposes. Counsel said that they had met with her along with the human resource director, and that the woman established a plan to pay the organization back for the charges. Counsel said the woman signed an agreement to repay the funds, and that the repayments were being withheld from her paycheck. Tim said the agreement brought to an end any further actions against the woman.

I asked if Tim or counsel had heard anything from the controller's attorney regarding the information he said they would provide. Counsel said a letter went out to the controller's attorney requesting the promised information, but that nothing had been received, and no response was provided. We agreed it was likely that nothing would ever be provided, as nothing likely existed that could legitimize the charges and activity. Counsel said if in fact the receipts and invoices did exist and showed the purchases were personal in nature, they would never be produced, as their production by the controller would only further implicate the controller.

Lastly, I asked about the status of the insurance claim. Tim said he followed up the claim with a voice message to the claims adjuster assigned to the claim. Tim said he hadn't heard back from the adjuster. I indicated he needed to stay on top of the adjuster to get the claim processed and paid, or it would sit until they got around to paying out on the claim. I said these claims are the types that you needed to call often about to keep the process moving, to ensure you receive your payment in a timely fashion. Tim said he would call again today and let me know the status of the claim.

Counsel thanked us for the update, and with that we ended the call.

CHAPTER 14

CASE CLOSED!

Several weeks later Tim called to tell me that he had just received the insurance check for $49,000 from the insurance company. He said he was happy another part of the puzzle had been completed, and that the matter was finally starting to wrap up. Tim said he was depositing the check into the division's account today, and would send me a copy for my files. I told him I was glad things were starting to come to a close on the case, because the longer these cases drag on, the longer the events remain on your mind. I asked him if he had heard anything from the detective regarding the status of the arrest warrant. Tim said he hadn't heard anything, but he would call and leave a message asking for an update. I asked him where things stood with the civil case against the controller. Tim said he had spoken with counsel earlier in the week, and that the case wasn't doing much. A subpoena had been issued to the controller demanding copies of the invoices and receipts, the same information he and his attorney had promised to provide but never did, but no response had been received. Tim said the civil case wasn't likely to gain ground until the criminal case heated up with the controller's arrest. I told Tim I thought he was right with his assessment. I asked him to let me know if he heard anything, and congratulated him on recovering $49,000 for the division.

The next time I spoke with Tim, he called me to let me know he had just spoken with the detective, and that the controller had been arrested. I asked Tim if he knew what happened. Tim said while he had hoped the detective would go out to the controller's house and arrest him, put him in handcuffs, and drag him down to the police station, all in front of his neighbors and other onlookers, it didn't happen in that fashion. Tim said it was actually quite uneventful. The detective told him he called the controller's attorney to let him know he had an arrest warrant for the controller. The detective arranged an early morning time for the controller to come to the station to be arrested. On that morning the controller came in with his attorney to be arrested. The detective said once he was processed, the controller's attorney posted the bail funds and they left the station. I told Tim I was disappointed as well and that I would have loved to have seen the controller marching up the front steps of the police station, handcuffed and surrounded by the media. I also told Tim that it almost never happens that way, unless the crime committed is egregious in some way, especially for financial crimes. I asked Tim what happens next with the case. Tim said he already provided a similar update with counsel, and that counsel was going to communicate with the controller's attorney to see if they now wanted to meet to resolve the civil matter. Tim said he hadn't heard back from counsel, but would let me know as soon as he heard anything.

Within an hour I received a call from the detective. He said the controller came in and was arrested earlier, and then left with his attorney after posting bail. I played along as if I hadn't already heard from Tim, and asked him what happened. The detective provided me with a similar story, and ended by asking me to keep the update between us. I agreed (and thought to myself, Tim likely agreed to something similar, although he already called me). I thanked the detective for calling, and asked if he knew when the next court date would be for the controller. The detective said he thought it would be around the end of the month, but wasn't sure of the exact date. I told him to let me know if he needed anything further.

Within a day I heard from Tim. Tim said he sent me an e-mail with a link to a news article he had just read. I opened my e-mail and scanned my inbox for Tim's e-mail. I opened it and clicked on the link. The following story appeared in the local paper:

CONTROLLER CHARGED WITH EMBEZZLING FROM NON-PROFIT AGENCY

James Smith, 43, was arrested yesterday on charges that he pilfered hundreds of thousands of dollars from his employer over the course of several years. Smith turned himself in to local authorities accompanied by his attorney after learning that police had secured a warrant for his arrest.

(Continued)

Smith started at Crestview as an accounting manager and rose through the ranks to become a controller. A surprise audit revealed Smith used the organization's credit cards for personal expenses in support of his lavish lifestyle, including trips he took throughout the world. Funds intended for Crestview were diverted into a bank account opened by Smith that he allegedly used to pay the credit card activity each month.

Shortly after the discovery, Smith was placed on administrative leave. As part of the negotiations for a potential plea deal, Smith purportedly agreed to initially return $78,000 and make restitution to Crestview for the full amount of their loss.

Smith was released on a $100,000 bond and is scheduled to appear in court next month on March 29th. No one answered the phone at Smith's residence, and messages left for his attorney went unreturned.

I asked Tim if he knew the case was going to be in the paper. Tim said he was contacted yesterday by a reporter asking about the case, but that he didn't return the voice message. Tim said he suspected if a reporter was calling, that an article was likely to appear. I asked Tim if any other articles had appeared, and Tim said he searched all the newspapers and found no others.

I asked Tim if he knew anything about the initial return of $78,000 and restitution agreement cited in the article. Tim said he didn't know about either, but knew that counsel had connected with the controller's attorney to begin discussions in the matter. I asked Tim if he knew who provided the information to the reporter. I told Tim I didn't know anything about any repayment arrangements or the article prior to his call, and that the only place the information could have come from was either counsel or the controller himself. I said I could see the controller saying things like that to mitigate and minimize the impact of the story, a self-serving statement if you will, perhaps to reduce the potential sentencing in criminal court if he showed the return of all the funds. Tim said he didn't know either, but was confident it wouldn't have come from counsel. Tim speculated if the information was provided by anyone, it would have come from the controller or his attorney.

EPILOGUE
DO YOU WANT TO KNOW THE OUTCOME?

The controller did appear in court on the 29th. It turned out the same reporter was at the court that day to snap a quick picture of the controller for the next article, should the outcome be newsworthy.

In advance of the controller's court appearance, counsel for the organization had met with the controller's attorney and the prosecutor to discuss resolving the case. Through those meetings the controller agreed to take a plea deal, which would conclude both the criminal and civil cases against him. As part of the plea agreement, the controller would not plead guilty, but would concede the state had sufficient evidence to pursue a criminal case and likely a conviction against him. The plea agreement included a provision for the immediate return of $78,000 to the organization. The controller would also be responsible for repaying the difference between the total loss plus investigative costs per my report, less the $49,000 received from the insurance company and the $78,000 paid up front. The repayment of the funds would occur to the organization over the next five years. The controller in return would avoid any jail time, and would receive a suspended sentence along with seven years of probation and 100 hours of community service.

The plea agreement did not include resolving recovery by the insurance carrier for their claim payment of $49,000 to the organization, as they were not party to the actions. Therefore, the insurance company would likely continue to pursue repayment of the $49,000 directly from the controller as well.

The controller accepted the plea deal, paid the initial $78,000 to the organization, and avoided jail. As much as everyone involved wanted to see the controller go to jail, I believe everyone directly involved in the investigation was satisfied that the case was successfully pursued and the organization recovered as much as it did. Now the organization could put the whole event behind it and focus on the future, with the hopes of implementing better controls and procedures to prevent similar things from happening again.

I knew that such outcomes were common in these types of financial cases, and as much as I hoped the controller would go to jail even for a minimal amount of time, I also knew the leverage in resolving these cases and returning the funds to the victim almost always led to the suspect avoiding prison. The controller received a felony conviction on his record, had to perform community service, and had to report to a probation officer regularly for the next seven years. All of these would be inconveniences for the controller. Not the ultimate goal of inconvenience via prison, but nonetheless, inconveniences he would have to deal with for a while.

I look back very satisfied that I did the best investigation possible, from beginning to end, and that my involvement was a big part of the reason the organization received nearly all of its funds back, something that seldom happens in these financial cases. I know my role was instrumental in nearly every aspect of the case, but it was the combined efforts of Tim, the senior accountant, the human resource director, and counsel that made the outcome such a success.

I found it interesting that the detective and the prosecutor never asked Tim for the original evidence stored and maintained in Tim's secured storage room at his building. We worked so hard to establish and maintain a strong chain of custody, documenting and preserving every step of the way, just as every case needs to be completed to ensure the evidence will be admissible, and yet we never provided any of that information, let alone the evidence itself, to be used in the case. Interesting.

With the case over, Tim and the rest of his coworkers in his building got their storage room back, and the hallway looked less like a crime scene once the evidence tape was removed from the entrance door.

At my firm, we were able to clean up our evidence room, box and seal all the records relating to the case, and burn CDs of all our electronic files. It was a good day for us, as we have limited secured storage space, and I, personally, look forward to clearing the room to make space for new cases. As quickly as a case clears, another is right around the corner just waiting to be detected. Then we start the whole process all over again. The process doesn't change much, only the facts and players specific to each case. With the sealing and archiving of the boxes of records, our role in the case officially ended. All our invoices were paid in full.

Case closed!

NOTES

Chapter 1

1. Association of Certified Fraud Examiners 2008 Report to the Nation on Occupational Fraud & Abuse.

Chapter 2

1. Site can be found at http://whistleblowerlaws.com/index.php.

Chapter 3

1. United States Department of Labor, Occupation Health & Safety Administration, at www.osha.gov/SLTC/workplaceviolence/index.html.

Chapter 4

1. Wells, Joseph T. "Lapping It Up," *Journal of Accountancy*, February 2002. Published by: American Institute of Public Accountants.

Chapter 5

1. "Ten Most Commonly Used Passwords Online," *PC* magazine, May 8, 2007.
2. www.lostpassword.com/quickbooks.htm.

Chapter 7

1. *Black's Law Dictionary*, West Publishing Company, 2004.
2. Graham, Michael H. *Federal Rules of Evidence in a Nutshell* 402 (3rd ed., 1992).

Chapter 8

1. Redhead, Philip. *How to Read Body Language*. Empower Solutions. A free ebook from ebookmetro.com, 2003.

Chapter 9

1. Layton, Julie. *How Handwriting Analysis Works*, at www.howstuffworks.com, Howstuffworks, Inc., an eDiscovery Company.

Chapter 10

1. "Infidelity at the Office/Workplace," at www.infidelityassistance.com.

Chapter 11

1. "Understanding HIPAA Privacy," U.S. Department of Health & Human Services, at www.hhs.gov.

Chapter 12

1. "Right to Discovery Regarding Expert Witness Trumps Attorney–Client Privilege," Mack Sperling, North Carolina Business Litigation Report, at www.ncbusinesslitigationreport.com, May 6, 2008.

Chapter 13

1. Revenue ruling 61-185, 1961-2 CB 9; revenue ruling 65-254, 1965-2 CB 50; *James v. United States*, 366 US 213 (1961), Ct. D. 1863.
2. Alcorn, Ernestine K. TC Memo 1969-751.
3. McLain, P. Michael. "Accounting for Sticky Fingers," *Journal of Accountancy*, Vol. 188, 1999.

ABOUT THE AUTHOR

Stephen Pedneault, CPA, CFF, CFE is the principal of Forensic Accounting Services, LLC, a local CPA firm in Glastonbury, Connecticut specializing only in forensic accounting, employee fraud, and litigation support matters. His technical expertise and intuitive investigative awareness have garnered him the respect of the legal, accounting, and law enforcement communities. As a result, Steve is called upon as a litigation expert on an ongoing basis and is considered a highly regarded member of legal teams.

Working in public accounting for over twenty years, Steve is a Certified Public Accountant (CPA), a Certified Fraud Examiner (CFE), and Certified in Financial Forensics (CFF). He has an Associate's Degree in criminal justice from Manchester Community College and a Bachelor's Degree in accounting from Eastern Connecticut State University, where he graduated Summa Cum Laude.

Steve's first book *Fraud 101* was published by Wiley Press. He is currently writing *A Practical Guide to Preventing and Detecting Employee Theft and Embezzlement* (Wiley) which will be available in 2010. Steve has authored numerous articles appearing in local and national publications. Business and student organizations request him to speak on a wide variety of subjects, including forensic accounting, fraud prevention, risk assessment, embezzlement, probate concerns, and other related topics. He is often referenced and quoted in articles appearing locally, regionally, and nationally.

Through his investigative work, Steve has examined frauds ranging from a few thousand dollars to amounts well in excess of $5 million. His expertise also lies in preventing and investigating embezzlements and financial statement frauds, evaluating financial disclosures in matrimonial and probate concerns, as well as other types of forensic accounting matters.

As an adjunct professor to the University of Connecticut faculty, Steve has authored an innovative course on forensic accounting that has been offered since 2008 as an online class within UConn's

Masters of Science in Accounting (MSA) program. The course provides an overview of forensic accounting, identifying the qualities and attributes required of a forensic accountant, and provides students with an approach and skill set to enable them to perform a forensic accounting assignment.

When Steve is not playing detective and finding the missing money, he enjoys spending time with his family. In addition, Steve volunteers as an EMT on a community ambulance service. He also contributes his time in support of his sons in the Boy Scouts and a wide variety of other community projects. Steve recently was elected to the Board of Directors of the Connecticut Society of CPAs.

INDEX